CRISIS IN IDENTITY.

CRISIS IN
IDENTITY

AND

CONTEMPORARY

JAPANESE NOVELS

by
Arthur G. Kimball

CHARLES E. TUTTLE COMPANY
Rutland · Vermont : Tokyo · Japan

REPRESENTATIVES
For Continental Europe:
BOXERBOOKS, INC., *Zurich*
For the British Isles:
PRENTICE-HALL INTERNATIONAL, INC., *London*
For Australasia:
PAUL FLESCH & CO., PTY. LTD., *Melbourne*
For Canada:
M. G. HURTIG, LTD., *Edmonton*

Published by the Charles E. Tuttle Company, Inc.
of Rutland, Vermont & Tokyo, Japan
with editorial offices at
Suido 1-chome, 2-6, Bunkyo-ku, Tokyo

Copyright in Japan 1973
by Charles E. Tuttle Co., Inc.

Library of Congress Catalog Card No. 72-91549
International Standard Book No. 0-8048 1090-7

First printing, 1973

PRINTED IN JAPAN

TABLE OF CONTENTS

Table of Contents

PREFACE

Although a considerable number of Japanese novels and short stories have been translated into English, very little in the way of analyses or other literary criticism is available. A few specialized studies on individual authors exist, but virtually nothing in terms of a thematic study covering a given period such as the post-World-War-II era under consideration here. Hopefully, this book will contribute to the improvement of this situation.

More specifically, the book is intended to encourage the reading, study, and appreciation of contemporary Japanese fiction and, through it, an understanding of Japan and Japanese culture. The various chapters, including the Syllabus at the end, aim to stimulate and encourage general readers and students to deepen their knowledge of the available literature. The Syllabus in particular aims to encourage the teaching of Japanese literature in the classroom, at both high school and university level, by supplying the teacher and student with study aids.

The book is based on an important and much-discussed contemporary theme, that of identity. This is, of course, only one of many possible approaches; for, as the reader may already know, Japanese literature is rich and diversified. The author, without apology, acknowledges his framework to be primarily that of Western critical assumptions and ideas, to say nothing of his own personal quirks. Hopefully, others will contribute their own insights and further the cause of intercultural understanding.

The author wishes to thank publishers who granted permission to quote material under their copyright.

ARTHUR KIMBALL

1

CRISIS IN IDENTITY

In his intriguing prize-winning essay, "Patterns of Alienation in Contemporary Japan," Munesuke Mita probes the sources of modern Japanese anxiety as they surface in the personal advice column of one of Japan's largest newspapers, the *Yomiuri Shimbun*.[1] His purpose, Mita says, "is to (a) describe the processes by which self-alienation determines the everyday existence of ordinary people and (b) draw a composite picture of the numerous factors which impinge on the life situation of contemporary man."[2] Mita's effort, in short, is an examination of the postwar Japanese quest for identity. In a country profoundly influenced by the doctrine of "non-recognition of the ego," whose citizens are inclined to identify with or even dissolve into the group, the quest is striking.

Taking as material 304 cases printed in the *Yomiuri* during 1962, Mita analyzes the causes and backgrounds of a representative sampling. In one case, a nineteen-year-old high school graduate finds himself frustrated and depressed by his situation. He has failed to pass the entrance examination of the college he desires and so must pass an additional year as a *ronin,* or "floating student," studying in hopes of succeeding in the exams the following year. But the father's income is limited and the family budget frequently runs into the red. The result is friction between father and son; guilt, tension, and anxiety for the entire family; and what the young man describes as "dark days" for himself.[3] Another case involves a twenty-eight-year-old white-collar worker who feels he has been "permanently shunted off the escalator to success" in the firm where he works. Somewhat passive in nature, he wonders if he can resolve his doubts by having a brother-in-law arrange a good marriage match for him. He feels miserable and gloomy.[4] In still another example, a thirty-two-year-old housewife finds life has "no meaning at all" because her irritable husband, after achieving a stable life and considerable status as a government employee, spends more and more time with other women, leaving the wife to grieve at home.[5]

What Mita everywhere implies and occasionally suggests, but leaves primarily for the reader to ponder, is far more significant than the analysis itself, for the appeals to the life-counseling column represent an urgent and often poignant reexamination of the current Japanese value structure. Each case is the search of an individual for ways to satisfactorily identify himself as to his role in life, his relation to others, and his obligations to society. And behind the private questions of private persons lie larger questions about the assumptions and criteria of social behavior, though the depressed writers of the dark letters are often themselves victims of stereotyped notions about happiness and success. Behind the high school graduate's distress is the assumption of an entire system, namely, that graduation from a name university—the more prestigious in the hierarchy the better—is the indispensable ticket to a well-paying job and, presumably, happiness. Implicit in the white-collar worker's fear is the idea that success is an escalator process with the spatially nebulous "up" as its goal. The machine metaphor appropriately suggests the non-human character of the assumption. In the housewife's lament is a fairly direct challenge to notions that financial security and job prestige can begin to guarantee happiness.

One of the more colorful and dramatic challenges to what Mita calls "values unessential to one's humanity" comes not from the newspaper advice column but the current vogue of communal living.[6] One can, of course, assume an attitude of amused disdain and say, "It's a passing thing." And indeed it may well be. Historically, many communes have been established and have collapsed, for any number of reasons. But such experiments are striking illustrations of their adherents' questioning of a value structure they regard as inadequate, non-essential, or even absurd. And what, one wonders, would result from a friendly pow-wow between a group of commune dwellers and a cross section of their more conventional city cousins where they vied to establish who was the "happiest"? Might not such a confrontation prove, in more ways than one, to be semantically embarrassing? The "free man of tomorrow," Mita says, "must participate in creating and practicing universal primary values."[7] And so he must. But what are these values? What is success? What is happiness? The Japanese too are asking.

And behind such questions is the still larger one, for the current Japanese quest is but part of the never-ending attempt of man to define himself. "What is man?" asks the Psalmist in one of the oldest Western cultural sources. And the complementary admonition, "Know thyself," has from olden times teased men of both East and West, whether in Buddhist reflection or Greek humanism. "Knowing" may mean rejecting the concept of self or, as in Shakespeare's testament, recognizing the awesome extent of ego-possibility. "What a piece of work is man," he has his tragic hero marvel, and in a brilliant literary embodiment spells out the conditions under which a man may soar to angelic heights or descend to demonic depths. But for the twentieth century the concern with identity is almost an obsession. A book of American short stories currently on the academic market suggests the emphasis. Designed for either text or collateral reading, the volume is entitled *Identity: Stories for This Generation*. There is little or no explicit connection between the stories and identity. The authors note in passing only that one of the ways the stories may be read is "for social documentation providing insight into who we are and what we value."[8] But their title, they know, will sell; it is "relevant." And it *is* relevant, pointing up, even though superficially in this case, the contemporary focus on an age-old concern.

For postwar Japan, the problem of identity is critical. The loss of the emperor as a divine symbol and unifying force is but one of the countless alterations which have transformed the Japanese psychic identity. Nineteen seventy marked not only the year of Expo and the renewal of the controversial security treaty, but the twenty-fifth year since the beginning of the American occupation and the host of westernizing changes it effected. Defeated in war, its major cities devastated by fire bombs, Japan is the only nation to have suffered the atomic bomb. And the Japanese are conscious of the need to redefine themselves, to establish an acceptable self-image for themselves as individuals, as a nation, and as an emerging power in the world community. In many ways they are new, different, westernized, modernized; in many ways they are old, traditional, oriental. "This 'I,' what was it?" asks the protagonist of Haruo Umezaki's short story "Sakurajima." "For thirty whole years since my birth, I had been attempting, you might say, to discover what this 'I' was."[9] The Japanese are asking the question, at times showing an almost painful self-awareness.

What then is a Japanese? A particular Tokyo tour guide regularly advises sightseers to look at the man-in-the-street. "See him smiling," he says. "Look at his happy face. Times are good. The Japanese are prosperous. They are happy." Or so they seem. And times are good, so good in fact that the Japanese, displaying that penchant which people the world over sometimes have for creating a sow's ear out of a silk purse, for turning their own assets into liabilities, now castigate themselves with the label "economic animal," as if to condemn the very prosperity which brings them smiles.[10] But an animal, if not quite human, at least has life and vitality. Even more alarming is the threat of dehumanization or "thingification" which results from the bigness which creates the prosperity. "When an individual has been cut off from the means of production and made a fixed part in a gigantic system of specialization," explains Mita in his essay, "he inevitably loses any sense of identification with society."[11] Thus even their spectacular rise to the status of a world leader in commerce has caused the Japanese to search with concern, for they now share with the other industrial giants all the identity-shaking features of bigness and complexity. In an article, "Running with a Purpose," newspaper columnist Masaru Ogawa criticizes his nation for lack of direction. "There is no doubt that Japan today is running like mad—at least in the pursuit of economic gains. It has increased its gross national product at a tremendous pace. But where are we heading? What are the goals? 'Ask my feet' would probably be the most honest Japanese answer," he says.[12]

The economic concern is directly related to the matter of Japan's world image. "The Ugly Japanese," laments political commentator Kazushige Hirasawa, is a worse epithet than "economic animal." He points out that Southeast Asian peoples (with whom some resentment over Japan's World War II militarism still lingers) often refer to Japanese as selfish, greedy, and arrogant. Distrust of the Japanese is growing, he claims, and cites as one of the reasons what he sees as a contradiction between Japanese criticism of the Viet Nam conflict and her willingness to profit from it financially. There is a "gap between Japan as seen by the world and the Japanese view of Japan," he says.[13] The image gap idea is sustained by numerous tourist-directed books which claim to disclose the real Japan. While many of them merely capitalize on the old stereotype of the "mysterious Orient," Ichiro Kawasaki's *Japan Unmasked* is a different matter. The former ambassador to Argentina (who lost his job over his outspokenness) charges his countrymen with numerous weaknesses, including immaturity and feudalistic thinking.[14] Such severe self-criticism may or may not be justified, but the fact that it exists and that many take it seriously shows the question of identity to be a matter of international consequence. Japan now expects herself, and is in turn expected, to be a world leader and helper, particularly to her sister nations in Southeast Asia. This guidance and aid must be cultural, economic, and political, not military, her present leaders insist.[15] Both Japanese and foreign spokesmen sound warnings about the danger of recurrent militarism, and intense political discussion presently focuses on such issues as the role of Japan's Self-Defense Force and the security treaty with the United States.[16]

This insistence on Japan's non-militant role suggests something of the trauma suffered by the Japanese psyche from the militarism of the 1930s and the subsequent defeat in World War II. A good example is the strife on the university campuses throughout Japan during 1968 and 1969. Almost obsessed by the fear of returning to anything resembling a police state, school administrators refused to call police to the campuses until the situation reached chaotic proportions. Dissenting students capitalized on this reluctance. The university problem is a complex issue, revealing the search for identity in a number of ways. In part, of course, it is the rebelliousness displayed in some degree by every generation, a repudiation of the past, an expression of the desire to be mature, independent, resourceful. On a more philosophical level, it is part of a near-universal protest against the secularization of man, a voicing, consciously or unconsciously, sometimes shrill and incoherent, of the fear that the atomic age will divest life of its mystery and man of his manhood. But for the Japanese in particular it deeply involves the "face" of Japan, the entire social structure of the nation and the problems of an educational system long overdue for reevaluation and change.[17] It is also a special search for guidelines by a generation which shares with young people of other nations the desire to develop an acceptable self-image apart from, though with some guidance from, the past, but which unlike most others finds the past era repudiated even by its elders. The militarism of the 1930s is unthinkable; to look further to the past is to be archaic. "Should women's college girls be like mothers of the Meiji era?" one frustrated student recently wrote on the wall of a strife-torn Tokyo private college.[18] This graffito has a message. The girl is asking who she is.

There is no more dramatic, nor ironic, example of a contemporary search for identity than the current problem in Israel concerning who is a Jew. The issue has complex social, political, and religious significance.[19] Japan has no comparable example, but there is, in the striking growth of the so-called new religions, another indication of the contemporary search for values, a seeking for past assurances in modern dress. Two examples are the Buddhist-based Soka Gakkai and Rissho Koseikai groups, which claim followers in the millions. The former sponsors Japan's third largest political party, Komeito, while the latter offers group therapy sessions as part of its modern appeal. Both are, among other things, attempts to link past and present, to draw upon tradition and yet remain relevant and up-to-date. Though they emphasize group identity strongly, in both a modern stress on the individual operates as a subtheme. They are efforts to meet the needs of a people whose past is rich, whose present is prosperous, and whose future is promising, but who, after all, need something more substantial than room coolers and color television to insure a healthy self-image.

Examples of popular culture like comic strips and cartoons, though sometimes overlooked, also indicate the contemporary search to determine what it is to be Japanese. The ever-popular *Sazae-san,* which has been likened to America's *Blondie,* suggests, when one examines the assumptions behind the humorous incidents, something of the image Japanese currently have of the mid-twentieth century housewife and domestic scene.[20] Sampei Sato's cartoons provide equally illuminating insights into the frustrations of the salary man, whether it is in trying to please the boss, cope with the hazards of speeding traffic, or survive the stresses of the rush hour on the trains.[21] In one example, the befuddled protagonist tries to kiss a girl dressed and starved in the Twiggy fashion. He closes his eyes and, to the girl's cries of "idiot," kisses a slender tree instead. Such light moments afford welcome and wholesome relief to the more serious self-probing, but even here the effort to discern and define what it means to be a modern Japanese is apparent.

To be a modern Japanese, however, is not to be al-together "modern." Most Japanese, probably like most Americans or Europeans, would be hard pressed to say just to what extent they have been molded by their past, or to what extent past values still control their decisions. Ruth Benedict's *Chrysanthemum and the Sword* is helpful in understanding the Japanese mentality.[22] The traditional Japanese concepts of obligation, self-sacrifice, and shame are different than those of an American, she points out, and they still affect, sometimes profoundly, the behavior of many people. The recent university strife again provides a dramatic example. Westerners were shocked to read of the suicides of a few noted Japanese professors who in taking their lives claimed responsibility for failure to resolve problems on their campuses. To most Americans, the university problem, even on a given campus, would seem so complex as to preclude any one man's taking such responsibility on himself. Quite ob-viously, these Japanese professors looked at it otherwise. Similarly, other psychological patterns from past tradi-tion continue to operate among the people, particularly those of the prewar generation.

But the changes have been great. The most important ideological change in postwar Japan was negative, say the authors of America's standard textbook on East Asia. It was "the destruction of the sociopolitical identity that had functioned as the basis of orthodoxy until 1945."[23] In its place is something new. "The new education, the con-sumer society, new economic patterns, the rise in the status of women, the slow advance of the conjugal family ideal, unionization, the pursuit of happiness, the new religious freedom, all can be seen as quantitative change along lines begun in prewar Japan. Yet the changes are not simply linear. Rather, the total effect is a new social configuration, a new way of life."[24]

One of the indicators of the complexity of the new way is the very term "identity." For better or worse, one can no longer define oneself simply in elemental terms like "male" or "female," "adult" or "child." One is expected to draw and quarter and then further subdivide oneself into innumerable bits of allegiance which, metaphysically glued together, make up one's "identity." A Japanese now may be not only husband, father, uncle, or grandfather, but Liberal Democrat, Socialist, or member of Komeito. More than eldest son, head of household, or go-between for a friend's daughter's marriage, he may be inner-directed, other-directed, old-fashioned, or new-fashioned. In short, he may identify himself in terms of various combinations of factors—geographical, political, economic, social, religious, psychological, family, home, or other. And one might, if he is Japanese, be specially tempted to associate himself with the institution where he is employed, as the custom of identifying on the telephone implies. "Hello, this is Mitsubishi's Mr. Tanaka speaking," one says, or, "Hello, this is Tokyo University's Mr. Suzuki." It's all part of one's "identity."

The word "identity," admittedly, is ambiguous and slippery, but it may well be a keyword of the times. Perhaps by its ambiguity it may suggest, as such ambiguous keywords often do, something distinctive about the age. Perhaps the passion for identifying, classifying, clarifying, and showing relationships is in part a measure of twentieth-century man's failures in the area of simply being. At any rate, the problem of identity is prominent in the minds of Japan's contemporary artists, and the postwar Japanese novel stresses the quest and sometimes hints at the goals.

In attempting to trace out such a theme, the Western critic should acknowledge the difficulties of the subject and the limitations of his approach. There is, first of all, the perennial problem of translations. Already a miniature battle of the books concerning the difficulties of translation into Japanese is available to readers of English in the form of journal articles.[25] Shoichi Saeki, commenting on the translations into English of Junichiro Tanizaki's *The Makioka Sisters,* Yasunari Kawabata's *Snow Country,* Osamu Dazai's *The Setting Sun,* Shohei Ooka's *Fires on the Plain,* and Yukio Mishima's *The Sound of Waves* and *The Temple of the Golden Pavilion,* says, "My experience, from the very first moment that I began to read the English versions, was a kind of shock."[26] This need not discourage, but it should caution the reader or critic to mind his characters.

He must also mind the fact that he operates with a set of critical assumptions and approaches which may be quite unlike those of the authors he sets out to study. Westerners often insist on a form or structural consistency which a Japanese novel may not exhibit. Edward Seidensticker comments about such "unshapen" examples, suggesting that a new literary category might be necessary to properly account for them. "One wonders whether a more embracing genre might not be established, without reference to the degree to which a particular work is fictional and perhaps given some such name as 'discursive lyric.' If so, it would embrace a great deal of what is most pleasing in Japanese literature, even if the best of that literature might have to be excluded. The genre would be characterized by the want of concern with over-all form and dramatic conflict and by a compensating emphasis upon a succession of lyrical moments."[27] One thinks of certain of Kawabata's works as partly within such a tradition. And one should note that the "I-novel" (*watakushi shosetsu*), or autobiographical fiction, has a long history in Japan and, though somewhat in disrepute in the West, it is one of the major motifs (some say the mainstream) of Japanese fiction. Further, there is a difference between the Western autobiographical novel and the Japanese "I-novel." "In the Western autobiographical novel," says Jun Eto, "the life of the protagonist is usually presented against a wide social background because the confrontation of the protagonist's self with his social and cultural environment is the fundamental problem for the author. On the other hand, the Japanese *watakushi shosetsu* is a genre in which the assertion of the protagonist's (and therefore the author's) *sensibility* or *passion* is the main point."[28] An awareness of such a difference could of course profoundly affect one's reading of a given work.

But when these and other apologies and allowances have been made, the novels and the identity theme, happily, remain. The identity theme in fact suggests that while the postwar Japanese novel may retain much that is Japanese, it also speaks to contemporary man, is relevant to his deepest preoccupations. Philip Roth's *Portnoy's*

Complaint, for some weeks America's best-selling novel in 1969, illustrates the currency of the theme. The book shows, among other things, the narrator's continuous struggle with his identity. There are other themes in the novels considered here, of course, and one could approach them in different ways. They speak of love, death, alienation, loneliness, hope, despair, tragedy, and triumph; the motifs are universal. Each of the novels could be thought of as representing a quest for affirmation, a search for a frame of reference that would confirm the worth of modern man. Thus, the troubled young high school graduate struggling to reach university might find his frustrations embodied in diminutive Bird, the hero of Kenzaburo Oe's *A Personal Matter.* Perhaps the problems he outlines in his letter to the *Yomiuri* will even find a solution through Bird's courage in quitting the academic world and achieving satisfaction through other work in a way which carries an implicit challenge to the assumption that a university diploma is the magic ticket to job and success. For the boy's father, approaching retirement on an inadequate income, the zesty lust for life of Tanizaki's mad old man may prove heartwarming; or he may find a different kind of consolation in the fellow-suffering of Kawabata's aging protagonist, Eguchi, in *House of the Sleeping Beauties.* A young woman who feels trapped by obligations to her parents and fears that life is passing her by may gain a sense of liberation from Osaragi's resourceful women in *Homecoming.* Or again, salary men, teachers, government workers, and others caught in the routine of the organization may find a kindred spirit in the estranged hero of Abe's *Woman of the Dunes.* As such persons join in the fictional quest, they will find pleasure, challenge, sometimes even medicine.

More often than not, the quest will be introspective. Due in part to the theories of Freud, Jung, and their followers, twentieth-century man will more than likely turn inward for the answer to who he is. The terrain of his search will be the landscape of the mind; the quest will be into the depths of his own consciousness, as it is for Eguchi, Niki, Mizoguchi, and Bird, the heroes of Kawabata, Abe, Mishima, and Oe. Under the particular stresses and strains of his time he may feel himself a schizophrenic victim, divided against himself like the troubled speaker of Theodore Roethke's poem, "In a Dark Time," who asks, "Which I is *I*?"[29] And having tunneled within, he may have to turn outward again, looking beyond himself for any certainty or affirmation. Rituals, declares Margaret Mead, are man's ways of showing that his humanity depends on the traditional wisdom of society. But what if the traditional wisdom should fail? "When men lose this sense that they can depend upon this wisdom, either because they are thrown among those whose behaviour is to them no guarantee of the continuity of civilization or because they can no longer use the symbols of their own society, they go mad, retreating slowly, often fighting a heart-breaking rear action as they relinquish bit by bit their cultural inheritance, learned with such difficulty, never learned so that the next generation is safe."[30] In Shohei Ooka's *Fires on the Plain,* the bewildered protagonist, finding indeed "no guarantee of the continuity of civilization" in his death-ridden surroundings, goes mad. He retreats into schizophrenic isolation. Artists, in pursuing the quest, sometimes find disturbing answers.

The quest begins at the war's end, "in a dark time." From defeat comes the need for redefinition. After the bomb drops and the paralysis ends, one must try to discover in past remembrances, present facts, and future unknowns some purpose for rebuilding. Masuji Ibuse's *Black Rain* directs one to elemental needs, suggesting that hope may be in the form of the everyday. For the self-preoccupied expatriate of *Homecoming,* however, such comforts are inadequate. He fails to find himself. The trapped man of Abe's *Woman in the Dunes* finds his existence a prison, but reduced to elemental considerations is able to reconcile himself to his fate. Kawabata's old man is not so fortunate; his attempt at symbolic escape ends in frustration. Mishima's alienated young acolyte in *Temple of the Golden Pavilion* reveals an artist's sensibility; his quest for freedom ends in ambiguity. Oe's version ends more positively. The hero of *A Personal Matter* discovers within himself the courage to fight; when he decides it shall be on behalf of others, he at last realizes who he is. But if the quest ends happily for Bird, it begins on a note of terror for the victims of the great war in the Pacific. In the Philippine jungles at war's end, dying soldiers see a way of life turn to nightmare, a holy cause turn to madness and disease. The quest for identity begins with all pretenses stripped away. Ooka's Private Tamura is the incarnation of a horrifying possibility. Could contemporary man, could a Japanese, be a cannibal?

2

THE WAR AND THE CANNIBALS

Fumiko Hayashi's short story "Bones" records a nightmare:

> The man woke up, aroused by his own cries. "Oh,
> I had a terrible dream," he said. . . .
> "What kind of a dream was it?" she asked.
> "Well, I killed a soldier. I killed a dying man . . .
> fried his flesh and ate it. . . ."[1]

The apparition haunts the Japanese literary imagination in the immediate postwar era. The Japanese, however, are not alone. A host of more or less illustrious literary witnesses, from Montaigne to Mailer, testify that cannibalism continues to provoke men to creative response.[2] On one level, the taboo-ridden specter of humans eating human flesh calls to mind primitive rites of identification, the eating of something to become like the thing eaten, a practice which persists symbolically in the Christian sacrament. On another level, the one most exploited by modern writers, cannibalism is an emblematic projection of the darkness of man's mind, of all that resists the civilizing conventions of society, an actualization of the savage, sexually assaulting, death-dealing potential we sometimes suspect, but may deny, lies within us.[3] At its dramatic worst, it is reversion to chaos, annihilation, the ironic vision of man consuming himself in an ultimate madness. Cannibalism, in the hands of the ironist, is a powerful theme, portraying man as glutton, rapist, madman, killer, and—under a compassionate touch—as man in need.

Part of the theme's shock value is that such an act, almost universally considered unnatural, can occur at all among modern, technologically advanced, "civilized" people. More jarring, however, is that modern man has provided the matrix, war, which generates the act. Wars and rumors of wars, from the "war to end all wars" to the current conflicts, give ample scope for commentary, and the frequency of the motif in twentieth-century literature is hardly accidental. For the Japanese who experienced the Pacific war, cannibalism has a special immediacy. Japanese troops trapped in the Philippines near the end of the conflict fled to the mountains and for agonizing months struggled desperately to survive. Some few, perhaps crazed by hunger, malnutrition, and disease, ate and, in their desperation, even hunted for human flesh.[4] Three postwar Japanese literary works confront the reality and record the shock. Tadashi Moriya's *No Requiem,* Shohei Ooka's *Fires on the Plain,* and Taijun

Takeda's *Luminous Moss* comment on man's confrontation with his man-eating self.[5] The result is intriguing and ironic. The emphases differ, but one message comes through clearly: man's unnatural—or all too natural—penchant for violence has fostered the conditions which foster the act. Indeed, in view of man's predatory instincts, eating is but the logical next step after killing; there may be little or no moral distinction between the two deeds. Hypocritically, however, men condemn the one and condone the other. The authors dramatize the inconsistency.

They are not the first moderns, or Asians, to protest. In 1918, when the last mustard gas was dissipating over the fields of Europe, Lu Shun produced his condemnation of traditional Chinese society, indicting through his shaman-like mad sage a culture whose history was "a record of man-eating," and where "everyone wants to eat others but is afraid of being eaten himself." The leader of the man-eaters around him, he finds, is his older brother. A still deeper awareness comes when he suspects to his horror that he too may have eaten flesh, that of his younger sister.[6] In similar fashion, Japan's entry into the modern, postwar literary era reveals a poignant soul-searching into the nature of man and society.

Mildest of the three books is Moriya's *No Requiem*. A more or less factual account, the story records author Moriya's life as an army doctor in the Philippines during the closing year of the war in the Pacific. According to the translator's preface, details of cannibalism were omitted in the Japanese original, but included in the revised English edition. The facts by themselves would be grim enough, with or without cannibalism, were it not for Moriya's genial tone and matter-of-fact acceptance of the events. A battalion of one thousand men is gradually reduced to fifty, mainly by disease and starvation; swollen and disfigured corpses are a common sight. Only a relatively dispassionate and low-keyed presentation could make "light literature," as the translator calls it, of such a subject. But the terror is played down, and the result is a very readable, though not emotionally demanding, account. It ends happily with the narrator safe in Japan, joyfully united with his family.

Moriya mentions several instances of soldiers eating human flesh. The first is "a weird story" brought back by some men who go to bury a comrade. When they remove the cloth which is covering the corpse, they are horrified. "He couldn't believe his eyes, Maeda said. The dead body of Kawaguchi had turned to a sheer skeleton in one night, the flesh cut off clean. At once he suspected the 'Japan guerrilas' of such infamous act" (p. 288).[7] These guerrillas, the author explains, were starving soldiers "hard put to it" to stay alive. "Extreme hunger had turned some of them to the living demons. They were driven to attack a solitary soldier and find the source of supplies of animal matter in the *Hominidae*. *Homo homini lupers!*" (p. 289). Though the reader may find this hard to believe, Moriya says, it is an undeniable fact of which he is ashamed. "I had to admit it when a Sergeant of the First Company was attacked by one of them and wounded on the thigh" (p. 289).

A soldier named Takahara reports the next instance. When he approaches a group of men cooking a meal, they try to hide the contents of the mess-tin. Takahara gets a look anyway. "A good deal of fat swam on the surface of stew they were cooking, and he saw at once it couldn't be the *karabaw* meat." Moriya follows this with two more examples. "Then I had the news that an officer of another unit was eaten up by his orderly as soon as he breathed his last. I believe the officer was so attached to his orderly that he bequeathed his body to his servant, and the devoted orderly faithfully executed the last will and testament of his lord and master, and buried him in his belly instead of the earth" (p. 290). The last evidence is the disappearance of a sailor who was returning to his hut ahead of his companions, carrying some of the carabao meat they had secured on a successful hunting foray. His disappearance is attributed to the Japanese guerrillas.

But though he cites the evidence, Moriya mitigates it in a number of ways. The "Japan guerrilas," for example, are "hard put" to exist, they are turned to demons by extreme hunger, they are driven to attack others by necessity. As the language suggests, the guerrillas too are victims, passive instruments of the wartime fate which controls them. Again, in the story of the officer and the orderly, the facts are softened by the author's attempt, though strained, at humor. Finally, Moriya finds a scapegoat in the military. Since the Japanese army in the Philippines had lost control over the troops, he says, "no surprise at all, if some of them had turned to the cannibals driven by a wolf in the stomach when they themselves were wolves by nature." The ultimate responsibility thus rests with the warlords. "For all these infamous brutalities the Japanese Army in the Philippines was absolutely responsible. Had they grasped the war situation accurately and taken proper measures to cope with it, casualties on the Philippine Front would have been far less. Nor would such a glaring stain of cannibalism have been imprinted on the history of Japan" (p. 291). One might well ask what sort of "grasp of the war situation" Moriya has in mind, but his attempt to fix the blame may be genuine, if unconvincing. He has, at least, tried to prepare the reader for this point of view by a number of moralizing asides blaming the Japanese military for the disasters he experiences. Thus ameliorated, cannibalism is portrayed as a mildly climactic event which is merely the inevitable worst of a series of desperate acts by desperate men. The reaction of "frozen horror" at the first encounter becomes, within two pages, "no surprise at all." If the reader has any second thoughts, he is left to indulge them on his own.

Fires on the Plain is a different matter. Like *No Requiem,* Ooka's narrative takes place in the Philippines during the close of the Pacific war; the protagonist tries desperately to keep from starving or being killed by the enemy Americans, hostile natives, and his own countrymen. Surrounded by the dead and dying, he spends much of his time searching for food. He eventually confronts the truth that men are eating human flesh. But the similarities, striking as they are, are less important than the differences.[8] *Fires on the Plain* is a metaphysical quest, and Private Tamura makes the dark journey, familiar to literary tradition, into his own heart of darkness. There is little doubt that spiritual as well as material food is at issue. Along the way he confronts death continually, agonizes over his identity, and probes the implications of a flesh and blood communion. The heart of hearts, in this instance, is a clearing in an otherwise dense forest where an unlikely trinity of three fugitives, Yasuda (Nagamatsu calls him "Dad"), Nagamatsu ("adopted" by Yasuda), and the troubled Tamura, live in mortal fear of one another. After killing Nagamatsu, who has killed Yasuda, Tamura loses his memory and wanders off. He is wounded, captured, and returned to Japan, where he endures a schizophrenic existence in a Tokyo mental hospital.

Moriya, the narrator of *No Requiem*, is never without companions who appreciate him. As a medical man he is respected and needed. Most of the time his talents win him favored treatment. In contrast, Private Tamura of *Fires on the Plain* is an unwanted outcast; his diseased and hungry body only repel people. From the opening lines he bears the curse of the condemned man. "My squad leader slapped me in the face. 'You damned fool!' he said. 'D'you mean to say you let them send you back here? If you'd told them at the hospital you had nowhere to go, they'd have had to take care of you. You know perfectly well there's no room in this company for consumptives like you!" (p. 3). Thus cursed from the community—such as it is—Tamura begins the lonely search for his salvation. His only "friendship"—the tenuous link with Nagamatsu and Yasuda—ends in violent death and psychosis. Moriya reaches home and the arms of his loved ones; Tamura a sanitarium, his wife in the arms of another man. Unlike Moriya's expression of joy, Tamura's is a pathetic claim to immunity from hurt. With Swiftian fervor he asserts,

"I don't care. Just as all men are cannibals, all women are whores" (p. 236).

Private Tamura's traumatic experience records the disintegration of a personality, the splitting of a self into selves with attendant psychotic confusion and frustration. The journey of discovery ends in madness. Ooka is putting the very concept "human" on trial. Early in his narrative Tamura notes the onset of the trouble: "Fundamentally, I suppose, my recent confusion of thought and feeling derived from the fact that the equilibrium between my inner consciousness and the outer world had begun to break down. This process had started when I was being transported across the ocean to fight and kill, and I suddenly had realized that I had not the slightest will either to fight or to kill" (p. 19). By the end of the novel he is obsessed with the problem of his identity and vacillates between his roles as "First-Class Private Tamura" and "an angel of God" (pp. 238, 242). Perhaps he has begun to internalize the external world; the madness of war has brought him to wonder if he too is meant to kill, ironically as a "destroying angel." Ooka provides considerable ironic depth and no little ambiguity for the record with his melange of Christian and Buddhist symbolism, descriptions of natural beauty, sexual reminiscences, and philosophical reflections on motion and "retrograde amnesia." At least part of the message, however, is clear enough. In an insane world, where death is the norm, where bloated, fly-ridden, mutilated corpses serve as caricatures of men, madness is the only logical response. When the life-process is inverted, when the community of men is a community of killers, the schizophrenic retreat is not only understandable but, ironically, the only appropriate action. Only madness can redress the balance.

The difference in the two books illustrates this point. The good doctor-author of *No Requiem* fills his narrative with quotidian details. If he notes the many deaths and hardships, he also provides the reader with numerous maps and charts which indicate even the sleeping positions of the men. Maps and charts are affirmations of order; they testify to locations and directions. One consults them to get his bearings. Perhaps even more reassuring are diagrams of shelters where even the locations of cauldrons, vegetable baskets, and mess-tins are considered worthy of mention. By contrast, the landscape of *Fires on the Plain* is dominated by images of death, from the darkly symbolic forests to the shattered corpses. When Tamura begins his journey, he enters the woods. "It was dark within the forest. . . . A death-like hush hovered over the enormous trees. . . . Here they had stood for decades and decades before I passed beneath them, and here they would continue to stand long after my death. . . . What was strange was the complete contradiction existing in my mind between the knowledge that I was passing here for the first time and the certainty that I would never pass here in the future" (p. 16). The gloomy forest and gloomy thoughts foreshadow the experience to follow, when death will dominate the scene. "Everywhere I saw bodies," Tamura recalls after an attack by enemy troops. "Their vivid guts and blood shone in the sun's rainwashed beams, while on the grass their severed legs and arms looked like the remains of so many broken dolls. Only the flies were moving" (p. 172).

And unlike the well-charted terrain of Dr. Moriya, the deathscape of Private Tamura sometimes becomes the nightmare projection of his own tortured psyche. "My next memory is an image of the forest seen from the distance. It was dark, like a Japanese cedar wood, and there was an insensate quality about the surroundings. It was hateful to me" (p. 224). Thus for the narrator of *No Requiem,* the external world retains a well-defined, objective validity, while for Private Tamura the world continually blends with his imagination, the mixture of dream and reality, vision and nightmare reflecting his troubled mind.

The religious theme gives ironic depth to the narrative. Attracted by the sight of a cross on a church steeple, Tamura, clutching his rifle, descends to the village to "resolve the religious doubt" that has visited him at the "end of his life" (p. 86). He has previously dreamed about the church, and witnessed his own funeral with a "coffin draped in black" where one of his selves lies, while another "I" observes the proceedings. When he reaches the village, images of death greet him. A "black swarm of carrion crows" perches on the church roof and arms of the cross; the church doors are black. At the foot of the church steps lie rotting corpses, "grotesque transfigurations of putrescence." Surprised by a young couple who have returned to the deserted town for a hidden cache of salt, Tamura murders the woman in the presbytery of the church, and adds one more "self" to his already confused identity. "I had to acknowledge that I was now no more than a brutish soldier who, far from being able to communicate with God, could not even mix with his fellow creatures" (p. 115–16). Private Tamura ends his curious confrontation with the Western passion symbol feeling that he no longer belongs to humankind.

Near the climax of the novel, Tamura encounters a dying officer crazed from suffering. The helpless man is covered with flies and leeches. As a symbol, the officer is an ironic composite, half Christ-figure, half Beelzebub.[9] Appropriately, when he offers his flesh to Tamura shortly before dying, the offer is a mixture of blessing and temptation. The analogy with Christ and the Mass is made explicit after the officer's death. "I remembered Jesus' arms, strained from hanging, which I had seen in the seaside village," Tamura says. But the demonic possibility too is suggested. "I was obsessed by the words that he had murmured before his death. For some reason these words, intended as an invitation, acted instead as a ban" (p. 184). Tamura's divided mind finds physical expression. His left hand seizes his right, and prevents it from using his bayonet on the dead man. After this experience Tamura has a strange religious vision (or hallucination) of an "unknown tropical flower" which says, "You may eat me if you like!" He then imagines great masses of flowers falling from the sky and hears what he takes to be the voice of God saying, "Consider the lilies of the field" (pp. 190–91). Much of the time he feels, as he has felt so often during his wilderness trek, that he is being watched. This feeling (do the "eyes" represent a projection of his guilt? a paranoid fear? a feeling of God's presence?) keeps the reader aware that the point of view here is that of a deranged mind.

The eyes finally assume human form in the person of

Nagamatsu, who rescues Tamura, revives him with water and what turns out to be human flesh (an ironic communion?), and keeps him alive until the climax when Nagamatsu kills Yasuda and is in turn killed by Tamura. The meaning of the religious motif is difficult to determine; the point of view (a sick mind) keeps one from being dogmatic. But part of the significance, at least, emerges from the ironic juxtaposition of redemption and destruction, feeding and killing, living and dying. Can these seeming opposites be reconciled? Can twentieth-century man, postwar man, with new and ever more sophisticated means of serving either end—eating or killing—find his role in his world? Can he count on divine aid? Tamura's religious yearnings are roused only when he faces death; when he confronts the crucified Christ (the crucifix in the church), he becomes a murderer. The profound import of the Communion gift of body and blood is only apparent (and then only to a distorted mind) when he sees that men must literally eat one another to stay alive. Perhaps the book's ironic possibilities are best summed up in the ubiquitous and symbolic fires on the plain. They suggest that man's response to his world may be natural or unnatural; they may be "genuine bonfires" for burning waste husks, or guerrilla signals to mark human targets. They may also be God's purifying fire of judgment. If so, then Tamura's last remarks are more than mere hallucinatory ramblings. Perhaps he speaks as an inspired shaman-sage, mad with the truth.[10] If man's insanity is somehow compatible with divine purpose, then indeed "glory be to God."

Like *No Requiem* and *Fires on the Plain*, Takeda's

Luminous Moss centers around an incident which takes place during the last year of the war in the Pacific. In an introductory narrative-essay, the author tells of his trip to Rausu in Hokkaido. Amid signs of postwar prosperity, he is guided to Makkaushi Cave, where he sees the famous "luminous moss." He also learns of a wartime incident of cannibalism which occurred in the vicinity. At the "apex of the War" a small ship had been wrecked in a storm; the captain and a crew member had straggled ashore on a "storm-driven, snow-laden beach." Two months later, the captain had appeared, sole survivor of the tragedy. But after fishermen had discovered evidences of cannibalism and the captain had confessed to having eaten his dead comrade, the "beautiful wartime drama" had become in the eyes of the people a tale of terror, the "courageous captain" a beast-like criminal. Author Takeda follows his essay with an imaginative recreation of the "incident" and the captain's trial in the form of a closet drama.

As in the other works, men, dying of starvation, resort to eating human flesh to stay alive. Like Ooka, Takeda has a symbol of the human heart, though more obvious, in the Makkaushi Cave. Both Takeda and Ooka get considerable ironic mileage from the identity motif and religious symbolism. But differences are again considerable. Whereas in *No Requiem* Moriya oversimplifies the problem of cannibalism (the Japanese military is blamed), and Ooka gives it a personal, mystical slant in *Fires on the Plain*, Takeda endeavors in a number of ways to universalize his message. He invites the reader to see himself, like the protagonitst, as Everyman, not only capable of, but deeply involved in, the act. Thus, Takeda explains that he chose the closet drama form of the play in order to "best allow the reader's everyday feelings to enter into and merge with the situation." In fact, the reader is invited to imagine himself as "producer" of the drama. Obviously, the significance is that one contributes not only in a literary but in a moral way. Lest the reader miss the point of his involvement, Takeda states the reader-producer analogy three times.

In other ways too Takeda stresses the involvement of all men. The introductory narrative has a peacetime setting with civilian characters, including the junior high school principal (his "educative" function becomes apparent when he is identified with the captain in act 2). Even the notorious "incident" involves not just military men, but "military civilians," and while the incident occurs at the apex of the war, the shipwreck results from a natural disaster, a snowstorm typical of the area, which could have occurred at any time. Allusions to Buddha, Christ, Bosch, Breughel, medieval Japanese scrolls, the Ainu, and contemporary Soviet-Japanese relations further stress the idea of universality. But most obvious of the universalizing devices are the symbolic luminous moss and the figure of the captain. In the "play," when Hachizo first sees the "ring of light, like the halo of the figure of Buddha" behind Nishikawa, he says, "They say—an' it's handed down from way back—that a man that's ate a man's flesh has a ring of light come out from behind his neck. A golden green light. A ring a pale, pale light comes out. Anyway, they say it looks like somethin' called 'luminous moss' " (p. 127). Hachizo's remarks point forward and back-

[38]

contains horror, for if none can see, then indeed
e thing is happening!" All are guilty, but igno-
eir guilt. But his words may also be an invitation
If the luminous halo is a symbol of sin, it is by
whether Buddhist or Christian, a mark of the
two are not incompatible. The Christ-like cap-
aring up" after all. Perhaps through the insistent
ne" Takeda suggests that if there is to be salva-
modern man, it must begin with recognition.
s moss" is then appropriately a symbol of il-
. The quest for identity begins with soul-

ward: forward to the play's end, where, in a crucifixion scene, the spectators all appear with halos of light, and backward to the introductory essay, where the narrator tells of going to find and of seeing the luminous moss. Since those who are themselves "human flesh eaters" can't see the light, by the end of the work nearly everyone (it's a closet drama, so the reader can't see the light either) becomes, as Takeda might put it, a producer. Takeda clearly calls for a moral happening.

As a composite Christ-Everyman figure (cf. Ooka's dying officer), the captain further points up the universality of human involvement in flesh eating. The Christ analogy is made clear in act 2 of the drama, which the production notes say is to have the atmosphere of a Passion Play. The captain's face is to be "like that of Christ" (as well as that of the junior high school principal). The spectators at the end of the play "look like the ring of spectators surrounding Christ as he was being taken to Golgotha for execution." As Everyman (as well as Christ), he is tried and convicted for the crimes of which all are guilty. His role is further suggested by the difference in his appearance between acts 1 and 2. In act 1 he is to appear as "the most sinister-looking man the reader can imagine"; in act 2, the "vicious look" is replaced by one of Christ-like calm, and he is identified with the angel-like junior high school principal and guide ("as he went on ahead of me, he made his lean body waver somewhat as if he were floating" [p. 97]). Perhaps the result is meant to be akin to what Renaissance writers portrayed so vividly: man's paradoxical ability to ascend to angelic heights or descend to bestial depths.[11]

The theme of Takeda's work is judgment, as the courtroom drama suggests, and Everyman is on trial. If *Fires on the Plain* stresses the journey to discovery, in *Luminous Moss* the journey has already been made, man's deepest secrets discovered, and the heart itself, accordingly, become the courtroom. The "producer" is invited to weigh the evidence of his own heart. The unspoken warning is "Judge not that ye be not judged." Takeda, at any rate, is blunt enough in his indictment of societies of men who condone war but pretend shock at cannibalism: "As a proud manifestation of the power of civilization, weapons of war and their mass production are openly displayed in the newsreels. Cooking utensils for human flesh, on the contrary, are no longer seen in the flatware sections of department stores or in the special exhibit rooms of museums. Of these two types of criminal tools, one has successfully won popular support and is being improved from moment to moment, whereas the other is about to be erased from memory as a secret weapon whose recollection sends a shudder of horror through the human heart" (pp. 114–15). The hypocrisy is pointed up with irony during the trial in the prosecutor's statement (greeted with applause) that "never must any comparison be permitted in the same breath between those loyal war dead who fought the hardest and starved to death for the sake of our country and this detestable, egocentric defendant!" (p. 136). Given the court's blindness, we thus find the captain, like Meursault in Camus's *The Stranger,* on trial for the wrong reasons. By act 2, the captain has thus become a scapegoat-Christ, bearing the sins of the world, not least of which is its refusal to acknowledge its motives.[12]

The central idea is bolstere
For example, Takeda capi
against the Ainu by subtle c
sion of the Japanese, he wr
only had fish but plenty of
content" (p. 95). Near the
for sacred music from a s
is, Takeda explains, "a w
expressing joy over bein
wish that the god retur
Since the music is hear
ceives the idea of murde
Ainu appear in anything
is the narrator's remar
Cave. He looks back an
footprints" left by his
comes a symbol of m
it's all over the place,'
National Treasures!"

But since the moss
needs a scapegoat vi
cannibal potential. In
condemn it, but will
For this reason the
"Please look at me
are both accusation
of course, to see hi
"fantastic creature
spoke. The truth
judge, prosecutor
light, all are by

plea thus
"a terrib
rant of th
to hope.
tradition,
saint. The
tain is "be
"look at n
tion for n
"Luminou
lumination
searching.

3

AFTER THE BOMB

It took Masuji Ibuse (1898–) over twenty years before he could properly defuse his own bomb, the one set ticking inside him by the great explosion at his birthplace in August 1945. But over two decades were necessary before he could articulate with his characteristic control, before he could set forth, with appropriate objectivity and aesthetic distance, the story he needed to tell. It is well he waited, for Ibuse is above all a stylist, relying to a greater degree than many of his contemporaries upon subtle contrasts, quiet touches of humor, and delicate shifts of nuance to carry his meaning. Of course more than aesthetic distance was involved. Ibuse's own identity was very much at stake. For one does not have to be melodramatic to assert that at least two generations of Japanese are not the same since the Hiroshima bomb. And Ibuse, with the added sensitivity that many Japanese feel for their place of birth, needed time to ponder, to sift through the details of the event, to evaluate, and to reevaluate again and again, what the world, Japan, and he himself had become and were becoming.

Black Rain evolves from a central gripping contrast.[1] Ibuse sets a single event, the atomic explosion at Hiroshima, against the ongoing, quotidian necessities of existence; a death-dealing, molecule-reordering destruction and recreation via discontinuity confronts a life-preserving, life-maintaining process of continuity. To what extent will the one bend, change, and reshape the other? How will the other absorb, counter, and amend the first? The novel grows from such unstated questions. In the lives of the characters, centering on the small family unit of Shigematsu, his wife, and his niece Yasuko, Ibuse portrays a way of life, capturing not only the full impact of the tragic event, but the resilience of the human spirit in response.

Something of Ibuse's achievement emerges when one compares the style of *Black Rain* with that of John Hersey's popular *Hiroshima*.[2] Hersey, Pulitzer prize-winning novelist and journalist, also had a story to tell; it is terse and dramatic. Six survivors of the blast struggle to comprehend what has happened to them. The reader follows, somewhat breathlessly, their alternating fates:

> "For we are consumed by Thine anger and by Thy wrath are we troubled. Thou hast set our iniquities before Thee, our secret sins in the light of Thy countenance. For all our days are passed away in Thy wrath: we spend our years as a tale that is told . . ."

Mr. Tanaka died as Mr. Tanimoto read the psalm.

On August 11th, word came to the Ninoshima Military Hospital that a large number of military casualties from the Chugoku Regional Army Headquarters were to arrive on the island that day, and it was deemed necessary to evacuate all civilian patients. Miss Sasaki, still running an alarmingly high fever, was put on a large ship. . . . Pus oozed out of her wound, and soon the whole pillow was covered with it. She was taken ashore at Hatsukaichi, a town several milies to the southwest of Hiroshima, and put in the Goddess of Mercy Primary School, which had been turned into a hospital. She lay there for several days before a specialist on fractures came from Kobe. By then her leg was red and swollen up to her hip. The doctor decided he could not set the breaks. He made an incision and put in a rubber pipe to drain off the putrescence.

At the Novitiate, the motherless Kataoka children were inconsolable. (pp. 79–80)

The style is that of the journalist, making the most of his dramatic material. The quick, restless pace keeps the reader on the proverbial chair's edge. The abrupt transitions continually jolt him. Repeatedly, Hersey ends the brief sections within his chapters on a dramatic, almost melodramatic pitch:

[45]

But then the doctor took her temperature, and what he saw on the thermometer made him decide to let her stay.

The priests concluded that Mr. Fukai had run back to immolate himself in the flames. They never saw him again.

He went to bed and slept for seventeen hours.

When he realized what had happened, he laughed confusedly and went back to bed. He stayed there all day. (pp. 72–73)

Thus end consecutive passages. Like a boxer's series of left jabs, they keep the reader unsteady and reeling. When he is properly "set up," the moral blow is landed. "The crux of the matter," Hersey states plainly at the end of his book, "is whether total war in its present form is justifiable, even when it serves a just purpose" (p. 115). Just to be sure, Hersey throws one last punch. A primary school child's report of the bomb furnishes the book's final words. "They were looking for their mothers," the child concludes, "but Kikuki's mother was wounded and Murakami's mother, alas, was dead" (p. 116).

Hiroshima was a timely book.[3] It furnished the English-reading West with a dramatic and exciting—but not too grisly—account of the event that terminated the war. It sold, and continues to sell, innumerable copies. Ibuse's work is of a different design, however, as the following quotation suggests:

A young woman who came along almost naked, with a naked baby, its face almost entirely covered with blood, strapped to her back facing to the rear instead of the normal way.

A man whose legs were moving busily as though he were running, but who was so wedged in the wave of humanity that he achieved little more than a rapid mark-time. . . .

Shigematsu had reached this point in his copying when Shigeko called from the kitchen: "Shigematsu! Whatever time do you think it is? I'd be grateful if you'd call it a day and come and have your dinner."

"Right! Just coming." Getting up, he went to the kitchen. He had been putting off dinner until now, staving off hunger while he copied out his journal of the bombing by munching home-made salted beans. Shigeko and his niece Yasuko had had their dinner long ago, and Yasuko, who was catching the first bus to Shinichimachi in the morning to go to the beauty parlor, had already gone to bed in the box room. (pp. 58–59)

Ibuse's ability to depict forcefully the horror of the bomb is clear, but equally clear is the fact that this is not his primary purpose. He does not long buffet the reader with descriptions of the victims without providing respite. The bomb is the central event, as countless delineations of the suffering and dying indicate, and gradually, from many points of view, a comprehensive picture of the events during and after the blast emerges. But the pace is leisurely, and interspersed with the record of the dead is the ongoing record of the living, of Shigematsu Shizuma and his family in their daily existence, writing, working, raising carp. When the dust—even atomic dust—settles, one must try to get one's husband out of his study, have one's hair fixed, catch the early bus, try to sleep. In this life-emphasis, Ibuse's purpose is not to shock nor to preach, but to portray the persistence of the human spirit. It is not a buoyant optimism; "black rain" is emblematic of an unspoken judgment, the judgment of a civilization upon itself, where a life-giving source is perverted into darkness. For such an indictment, the thwarting of young love is a an appropriately damning mark, and it is no accident that the tragedy for Shigematsu's household is the denial of marriage to the radiation-diseased Yasuko. At the end of the novel Shigematsu's carp pond is teeming with young life, but there will be no offspring for the dying young girl.

And yet Ibuse is ultimately affirmative. *Black Rain* states a philosophy, says translator John Bester, which "in its essence, is neither pessimistic nor optimistic," but which "seems to me to be life-affirming" (p. 8). What makes it seem so are Ibuse's stylistic techniques, by which he places the atomic event within a setting of timeless values. The result for the reader is a sense of emotional equilibrium and perspective. This is no small achievement. One of the techniques is the adoption of a relatively low-keyed tone. As anyone who has journeyed through the Hiroshima A-Bomb Museum can attest, the contemplation of the event, recreated in fine detail, troubles the heart. After reading the description of the bomb's epicenter and maximum heat, seeing the scale-model of total destruction in the city, and beholding the outlines of human flesh scorched into stone, one leaves feeling disturbed, depressed, or in tears. But in *Black Rain*, descriptions of the bomb's horrors, though vivid and realistic, are tempered in a number of ways. They are related in a matter-of-fact manner, they are accompanied by sensitive, thought-provoking observations, and they are juxtaposed with very human, ordinary, and sometimes even quaint actions. Ultimately, the reader focuses not on destruction and death, but on the life—common, everyday, cantankerous—which endures the destruction.

Thus, though one encounters the subtly horrifying simile which likens an injured boy's swollen face to a football, one soon reads with amusement of Shigematsu's attempts to "get a grip on himself" by picking up a stick and beating himself "indiscriminately" on the calves, buttocks, thighs, shoulders, and arms, and that the action gives him back control of his legs "as well as a certain mental detachment" (pp. 50,55). Or the frightened, sensitive Yasuko, watching the strange mushroom cloud, records in her diary that her knees shook so uncontrollably that she "pressed them against a rock, heedless of a small white flower clinging to it" (p. 22). Or again, one's horror at the thirty-year-old woman's bundle on the train—a dead child—soon shifts to the bellow of the man outraged by the train's lurching and stopping: "What the hell're you up to? . . . Ladies and gentlemen, you can see for yourselves how sadly decadent the National Railways have become. Concerned only with carrying black market goods, they have nothing but contempt for the ordinary passenger" (p. 114). And yet again, Mrs. Iwatake brings to mind the old Western folk tale of the princess and the pea when she recalls good-humoredly her husband's attempts, when he was near death, to try to go to sleep. Though they had "piled the quilts up high, as high as a bed, and put two feather mattresses on top," she records, her husband could still feel a slight bulge in the bedding caused by a joint in the tatami matting underneath, and couldn't fall asleep (p. 264).

The latter two examples suggest another of Ibuse's stylistic devices, the use of humor. When Shigematsu and Shokichi go carp fishing during the busy season on the farms, a jealous widow chides them. "Both fishing, eh? Some people *are* lucky, I must say, seeing how everybody else is so busy." After a spirited exchange of accusations and counter-accusations, the woman bites again. "Isn't that just what I'm saying—that it's very *nice* for you? That's why I said you were lucky." This unhinges the exasperated (and more than a little defensive) Shokichi, who splutters, "Why, you damned widow bitch!" (pp. 28–29). Shigematsu and his wife also provide humor. When they find some old tobacco leaves and Shigematsu asks his wife, Shigeko, why she didn't tell him about them during the war when tobacco was scarce, she replies that they were dry and that after all to have cut and smoked them would have violated the Monopoly Law. Shigematsu retorts, "Well put, woman! Why, you're as cut and dried as these tobacco leaves yourself! Aren't you, now?" (p. 42). Later Shigematsu and Shigeko discuss the difficulties with his journal in familiar husband and wife fashion:

> "I haven't got down on paper one-thousandth part of all the things I actually saw. It's no easy matter to put something down in writing."
>
> "I expect it's because when you write you're too eager to work in your own theories."
>
> "It's nothing to do with theories. From a literary point of view, the way I describe things is the crudest kind of realism. . . . By the way, have these loach been kept in clean water long enough to get rid of the muddy taste?" (p. 60)

Shigeko herself adds to the humor in her account "Diet in Wartime Hiroshima" with homey observations. One of them concerns the neighbor's wife who regularly took "a couple of ant-lions in a cupful of cold sake" to ease the headaches suffered because of the change of life (p. 70).

Mention of the ant-lions points to yet another of Ibuse's stylistic devices, the use of "digressions," particularly those concerned with quaint or traditional Japanese customs. Their presence partly accounts for Ibuse's often being ranked with Kawabata as one of the "most Japanese" of writers. The student of Japanalia will find *Black Rain* a surprise happening in this respect. Thus, Shigematsu discovers in a storehouse a treasured old letter of his great-grandfather's from a Meiji government official. In it the man thanks the great-grandfather for "two ounces of *kemponashi* seeds," and says he will recommend using the noble trees for lining the avenues of the capital. The letter evokes memories of traditional things for Shigematsu and he decides to rewrite his "Journal of the Bombing" using a brush and Chinese ink (p. 44). What seems at first to be a digression provides contrast with the descriptions of Hiroshima's devastation, reveals Shigematsu's sensitive, nostalgic nature, and delicately suggests the subtle nuances of feeling between Shigematsu and his wife, who had earlier suggested he use the traditional writing-brush ink.

Or again, in his postwar village home, Shigematsu performs the traditional chores required of the head of a farming household on an agricultural festival day. He washes all the tools, sharpens axes and sickles, weeds around the family shrine in the corner of the garden, and even goes to "pay homage" at Shokichi's carp pond for good measure. In another incident, Shigematsu attaches his wife's essay "Diet in Wartime Hiroshima" as an appendix to his journal, and then sets off to a friend's house with rice dumplings to celebrate the Mass for Dead Insects. This is a rite, he explains, in which farmers would "make rice dumplings an offering to the souls of the deceased insects they had inadvertently trodden on as they worked in the fields. On the same day, custom also demanded that they should return any articles that they had on loan from their neighbors" (p. 71). The subtle irony here is that the incident follows Shigeko's "Diet" essay, which ends with the observation that "war's a sadistic killer of human beings, young and old, men and women alike." Ibuse here juxtaposes a traditional custom of restoring the natural and domestic orders with an account of their destruction by war. Again, at one point Shigematsu has Yasuko pull out three hairs from the back of his head to help ease his nosebleed (p. 104). But whether he indulges such whims or joins his cronies in the carp-pond project, one gradually recognizes in and through him not only a particular character and his family, but a way of life which faces up to the exigencies of the moment responsibly and with equanimity. Confronted by much that is negative, the Shizumas affirm the continuity of their lives: the past through observance of custom, the present by insistence on the importance of daily chores, the future through Shigematsu's meticulously kept journal.

Ibuse's careful control over point of view also contributes to the affirmative tone. He begins and ends his novel with a relatively detached, third-person account— "For several years past, Shigematsu Shizuma, of the village of Kobatake, had been aware of his niece Yasuko as a weight on his mind. . . . So he told himself, with his eyes on the nearby hills, though he knew all the while it could never come true" —quietly leading into and as quietly withdrawing from his narrative. But a reader is soon drawn into Shigematsu's world, the lure in this case being the various first-person accounts, especially Shigemetsu's journal, of Hiroshima during and after the bomb. The narrative within a narrative is an old but effective literary device for involving the reader if it is used skillfully, as it is here. Ibuse adds complexity, and subtly involves the reader yet further, by using still other accounts: Yasuko's diary, the separate recollections of Mr. and Mrs. Iwatake, and Shigeko's essay "Diet in Wartime Hiroshima." They are all grist for Shigematsu's journal, as are the other individual narratives, such as when Shigematsu meets Mr. Miyaji, hears his adventures, and records them along with his own experiences of the day. The shifting narrative, registered through Shigematsu as the central intelligence, has several effects. Besides involving the reader, it creates a sense of realism. In fact, Ibuse has used interviews and adapted real diaries and journals, so that, as translator Bester suggests, the novel is in this respect a documentary (p. 6). The various narratives of the same event also establish a perspective. The atomic explosion filters through not one, but a number of observers, so that one develops a kind of communal consciousness, or sense of the whole, which mitigates any feeling of individual tragedy. Further, this collective sense keeps the reader aware of the scope of the event. The circle of people grows, and Ibuse's shifting accounts, humor, digressions, and tempered descriptions, unlike Hersey's staccato flurry of emotional punches, present not only Shigematsu's family but the sense of a community in its ebb and flow of emotional response to the introduction of chaos.

Ibuse's structuring of *Black Rain* provides thematic unity and reinforces the reader's feeling of ongoing life which balances Yasuko's tragic illness. The use of time is particularly significant. Shigematsu, unlike the protagonist of Abe's *Woman of the Dunes*, remains aware of time. He meticulously records the days following the explosion, adding the faintly ironic touch of daily weather commentary: "August 8. Fine and sweltering." But in other ways the temporal is subsumed under the timeless. The first and last sentences of the novel attest to Ibuse's time-consciousness. "For several years past," the book begins, thus setting Shigematsu's life at an undefined distance in time from the atomic explosion of August 1945. "Never" is the ominous reference at the end; never would Yasuko be cured. But between them the narrative shifts back and forth in time, from the journal records of August to the undefined present and the daily activities of Shigematsu and his friends. The result is a kind of interpenetration of the temporal and timeless, the memory of the bomb investing Shigematsu's life with an awesome presence, and yet Shigematsu's life investing the bomb with a new significance.[4] The "several years" between Shigematsu's present existence and the events of the bomb soon become blurred. To be sure, the events at Hiroshima are not to be forgotten, as Shigematsu's preoccupation with his journal attests; the journal, in fact, is to be presented to the public school library and thus preserved. But the journal, written at the time of the explosion, is being rewritten, one remembers—a bit of authorial sleight-of-hand which tends further to blend past and present. Timeless necessities—eating, sleeping, working—and the never-to-be-forgotten moment merge. Shigematsu's careful observance of the lunar calendar points up the subtle blend —timeless customs, observed in time.

Other major themes also unify the novel. Central, of course, is the terrifying explosion, its aftereffects, and the reaction of the people. The bulk of the narrative consists of detailed accounts of the days following the bomb. Shigematsu's journal includes descriptions, conversations, personal accounts, official notices, and even Buddhist scriptures. It ranges from the momentous to the insignificant. Sometimes the accounts are disturbing: "The skin of his back had come clean away from his shoulders, and was hanging limply, like a piece of wet newspaper" (p. 79). Occasionally they are thickly ironic: "On the main road on the way from Koi to Furue, we saw a dark brown, life-size figure of a man set up as a scarecrow in a tiny vacant lot being used to grow millet. . . . But Mrs. Doi said, 'It gave *me* a proper turn. I thought it was a *real* human being all burnt black'" (p. 19). More often they are ordinary, circumstantial, even trivial: "The one-and-a-half pint bottle was still one-third full. Should I drink it or not? I took out the cork, smelt it, put the cork back again, went to the kitchen, and was looking for a glass when an air raid alert sounded" (p. 286).

Throughout this life-size picture, a life-size man emerges. Shigematsu Shizuma is unobtrusive, a character whose significance a reader only gradually realizes. He is Mr. Average (though obviously, in good Henry James fashion, of above average intelligence), a contemporary Japanese Everyman, the familiar twentieth-century anti-hero, the ordinary man caught in structures and events too big to fully comprehend. He bears the marks of his initiation into the mad modern world (the radiation burns on his cheek), but, quietly persistent, he continues to affirm his place in the cosmic scheme of things. When during the emergency dead bodies accumulate and create a health hazard, Shigematsu's employer appoints him to "take the priest's place and read the service whenever there's a death" (p. 132). He accepts this near-heroic role with reluctance, though he performs dutifully and efficiently. Ibuse may or may not intend any special meaning here, yet just as Shigematsu recites to the dying victims the consolation of the "Sermon on Mortality," so he mediates to the reader in an unspoken way the affirmation of his own resilient spirit.[5]

Yasuko's fate is a different matter. If Shigematsu's hardy persistence is a positive theme, its somber counterpart is his niece's struggle against the effects of the death-dealing bomb. *Black Rain* is her story as well as Shigematsu's, from the opening sentence where she enters as a "weight" on her uncle's mind, to the final ominous words which reveal the hopelessness of her case. Denied a husband and her health, Yasuko remains the severest indictment Ibuse could levy against the modern world, for she is representative of the new generation, the future toward which each age looks in hope. Perhaps the gossip and rumors circulated by the Kobatake villagers represent not only that universally acknowledged community malice, but a projection of community fear and guilt, an implicit confession of the contemporary era's failure to love.

But even Yasuko's grim story is tempered somewhat. The medical reservist, Iwatake, one recalls, makes a miraculous recovery. "His body had shrunk to a mass of skin and bones, his fingers had fused together, and maggots had eaten away one of his earlobes. Yet he had come through. Plastic surgery had even restored his fingers to normal. Today, he was working as a general practitioner at a place called Suzaki-chō in Mukōjima, Tokyo" (p. 237). Ibuse thus preserves side by side the heroics of the living and dying, the tragically diseased and the magically healed. It is a moving portrait, created from a skillful blending and balancing of themes.

Not least in importance among them is the carp project of Shigematsu and his friends. The motif is introduced early in the novel after the men encounter the jealous widow who chides them for fishing. "For a while, Shigematsu and the other two gave up any idea of going to the lake to fish, but at Shōkichi's suggestion they decided to get together to rear carp in the lake. 'I'm so eager to give the woman at Ikemoto's a taste of her own medicine,' Shōkichi said, 'that I thought up the idea just to be nasty'" (pp. 31–32). But surely the project means more. Half-jests aside, the significance is several fold. When grown, the carp will provide food and recreation, both necessities. Meanwhile, and perhaps even more important, they furnish a goal, a task, a "project"—a projection of their own inner spirit. For Japanese, the carp is an old and well-known symbol of strength, ambition, and the will to overcome difficulties.[6] Like their Western counterparts, the trout in Hemingway's "Big Two-Hearted River," Shigematsu's carp suggest affirmation, hope, and the kind of balance which characterizes *Black Rain* itself.[7] At the novel's end, Yasuko is without hope; no miraculous rainbow will appear. But the baby carp are thriving. "The [baby carp] were coming along well, and in a shallow corner of the larger pond some water weed was growing. . . . Its oval, shiny green leaves dotted the surface of the water, and from their midst rose a slender stalk on which a small, dark purple flower was in bloom" (p. 300).

Perhaps the delicate balance of the themes is, ultimately, Ibuse's most powerful statement. *Black Rain* too can be seen as a quest for identity, the search of a man, a community, a nation—at a time when the world is obviously out of balance—for the balance necessary to preserve sanity and sustain life. To date, the explosion at Hiroshima is the twentieth century's prime emblem of technological advance, and also of human regression—the failure of men, once again, to live in peace, tending their carp, promoting marriage and a concern and reverence for life. But there is a solidity about Shigematsu that reassures. The opening sentence of the book (so important in so many ways) underscores it. For Shigematsu—for the Japanese— "obligation" has a resonance unfamiliar to Westerners; it radiates complicated but meaningful patterns of indebtedness and relationship.[8] The burden Shigematsu has assumed, namely, his niece Yasuko, is a "double, or even a triple, liability," but one gradually sees that he can shoulder it. There is a measure of comfort here, for the burden is everyone's. If *Black Rain* must *mean* something, if one is to indulge the Western penchant for finding a "message," then that message might be the quiet insistence that in the midst of discarding worn-out, damaged, science-blitzed, or no-longer-understood creeds and frames of reference, even amidst the violent reordering of existence, one must not allow the modern experience to bury the minute and daily. To find one's identity in the essential meaningfulness of daily life may be the only way of redeeming the time.

4

IDENTITY LOST

When Johnny comes straggling home—to a war-torn, devastated home—he must find himself anew. So must the disillusioned expatriate. For both, the return will be a challenge. Jiro Osaragi's *Homecoming* illustrates both these facts.[1] The novel has been damned with faint praise on two counts: critics frequently consign both book and author to the limbo of "popular" literature, and the novel is often dismissed, appealing though it may be, as another of the "glimpse into the soul of postwar Japan" works.[2] But these critical evaluations fall short of the mark, and a recent claim that "the main theme of Osaragi's *Homecoming* is a reappraisal of Japanese culture by an expatriate returning home after several decades abroad" is also inadequate.[3] True, the novel deals, at times quite sensitively, with the changes of postwar Japan, but more crucially central to the novel is, once again, the protagonist's quest for identity. The hero this time is an alienated man, Kyogo

Moriya by name, who joins the outsiders of Camus, Grass, Lagerqvist, Salinger, and others so familiar to contemporary literature in his search for a place and role in society.

But Osaragi's hero is a particular brand of alienated man. He is more "goat" than hero. In fact, he is a kind of self-appointed scapegoat. "I've been punished like the Wandering Jew," he says near the beginning of the novel. Near the end he asserts, "To be sure, wherever I go, I shall be alone again, living among people who have no interest in me. When I open my eyes in the morning, I shall be alone. When I go walking outside, I shall be alone. And at night I shall go back to my room alone, to sleep in my cold bed" (pp. 41, 296). He is right, but only because he wants it that way. The punishment is self-inflicted. At times he seems dimly aware of the real problem. Japan is "a narrow country," he tells the beautiful Saeko in the book's final scene; by living abroad "I can avoid emotional complications . . . and accept my own loneliness without deceiving myself" (p. 295). Not without deceiving himself, we are forced to correct. Moriya has rationalized and romanticized his failure to accept himself in any role but that of a kind of mythological martyr-hero.

In the mid-twentieth century, this mood of self-indulgence is all too popular; many readers will no doubt quickly identify with the handsome, unfettered hero who gambles his sad way through life. The underlying problem—lack of self-acceptance—is disturbingly common, perhaps universal. "Social change has rendered obsolete the traditional means of satisfying the self-needs, and no new tradition has evolved to fulfill industrial man," say social psychologists Snell and Gail J. Putney.[4] For Osaragi's protagonist, the setting in postwar Japan merely intensifies the problem. Kyogo Moriya is a romanticized version of twentieth-century man—afraid of emotional involvements. The reader shouldn't be surprised, then, to find the deck stacked by the author in the final gambling scene. Unable to accept himself, to forgive himself, and consequently unable to find—except for others—a satisfying role in rebuilding postwar Japan, Moriya wins a card game and makes his lonely exit, psychologically safe in his floating freedom.

The identity theme is introduced, somewhat dramatically, early in the book, when Moriya is imprisoned in Malacca by the Japanese. A young M.P. tortures Moriya and, infuriated by the older man's calm strength, loses all control: "You're Japanese! Japanese! Japanese!" he screams. Trapped in the confines of his cell, Moriya is forced to reflect: "The white backs and little hands and feet of the unmoving lizards on the ceiling soothed Kyogo's excitement now. 'He was right, I am Japanese.' He was murmuring out loud, half delirious with his fever. Clearly, he was Japanese, but a different sort of Japanese, who hated the madness of the torturer" (p. 54). Moriya obviously cannot identify with the hysterical nationalism caricatured in the young M.P., but the incident raises the issue.

After the war ends, Moriya is released from prison and decides to return to Japan. When he tries to explain his plans to his surprised Chinese friend, Yeh, he reveals his ambivalence toward his country and any role he might have there. "As a matter of fact, there's nothing I can do, I realize that, but still—I suppose it's because I was Japanese once. . . . I just have to go back, anyway." Yeh shakes his head disapprovingly. "You?" he asks in disbelief. Moriya changes his explanation. "I have a wife and child in Japan. I haven't seen them for years," he says. "Oh! In that case, it's all right," says Yeh, finally convinced (pp. 67–68). But the exchange is ironic, and Moriya's replies are only partial truths. There *is* much he could do in Japan, for Japan represents a challenge on several levels: his abandoned wife and child, Japan's future, Saeko Takano, and his own self-image.

These challenges, with the exception of Saeko, confront Moriya during his meeting with ex-admiral Ushigi, a scene crucial in the development of the identity theme. Here the protagonist's ambivalence concerning himself and Japan is portrayed with considerable irony. The two old friends meet in what Moriya acknowledges is "a really Japanese spring," and the traditional enchantments move him to respond. "I had forgotten," he sighs, "or rather, I never really saw it before—how beautiful the cherries are"; he finds himself "drawn to the relics of old Japan" (pp. 106–7). When they visit the Temple of Perfect Awakening and then discuss how the temples of Kyoto and Nara have been spared, Moriya says, "When you've lived abroad without kith or kin for twenty years, and you come back and grope for something that will bind you to your country's soil—It was a complete surprise to me. I don't believe in the gods or Buddhas. What power have these old shrines and temples that they draw me so? . . . Strange that an expatriate like me should feel this way—as though I were seeking somewhere to rest my soul and to breathe in peace." But Ushigi's reply quickly penetrates beneath the surface of this nostalgic and sentimental self-questioning. "Have you been to see your wife and family?" he asks bluntly (pp. 107–8).

Moriya maintains his calm, for the moment at least, and says, "I'll save my feelings for the landscape, not for people. . . . After all these rootless years the very idea of home has vanished from my mind." When Ushigi says, "I'm sorry for you, Moriya," the latter replies, "Don't be absurd. I have no intention of giving way to my feelings. I have some affection for others at times, but I know I can't expect anything in return. That's how you get to feel, when you've been wandering about in foreign countries all alone. . . . Why is it, why are the lonely hated? It makes no difference whether you're Japanese or, let's say, Persian. Alone in Europe, and you're bad. Why?" (pp. 108–9). Moriya here projects his own self-accusation. As he dimly suspects, the issue transcends national boundaries. His claim to be immune to his feelings is thus again only a half-truth, and in fact the conversation with Ushigi gradually unnerves him.

Moved by the talk of family and loneliness, Ushigi again inquires about Moriya's family. "You say you haven't been to see your wife and daughter yet? Don't you even love them?" he asks. Moriya's reply again suggests his self-alienation. "Love them? Why yes, I do. But you know how I am, I don't want to make the first approach." Ushigi's charge of "lonely fellow!" finally provokes Moriya, who reveals his defensiveness by shifting to the attack. "No. You're the lonely one. You doted on your son, like the Japanese father you are, and now—you've killed him in your war. You must really be lonely." The verbal blow hurts, for Ushigi is already burdened with guilt over his son's death. But it gives Moriya a temporary refuge behind the part of himself that can't identify with a militant Japan. Now psychologically one-up on his old friend, he presses the attack and rebukes Ushigi for his self-pity, inactivity, and for "still carrying death around" on his shoulders. "You've managed to save your life, and you don't even value it. You're sulking," he charges. "Why can't you shake off death and try to live?" (pp. 110–12).

At this moment, the two men appear strongly contrasted: Ushigi is withdrawn, weak, and full of self-pity; Moriya seems vigorous and self-assured. "You're just curling up small inside your shell, too frightened to look outside," he says to Ushigi. "You sulk and wish you were dead, but that only proves you don't feel capable of living" (p. 116). Japan needs men who will live not in the past but in the present and future, Moriya realizes, so he urges Ushigi to find work. But the confrontation of the two friends is full of irony, for there are as many similarities as differences between Moriya and Ushigi. During their exchange, Ushigi becomes a kind of alter-ego for Moriya, someone to whom he can attach his innermost thoughts. For example, at one point, when angry with his friend, Moriya muses: "And, strangely, his anger didn't seem to be on his own account, though Ushigi was hurting him. He had suddenly seen exactly what it was that made Ushigi like the young M.P.—the inability to feel the unhappiness of others. Ushigi was a fine man, of course. But a man out of the past, out of a Japan that had died already. And he sat there facing today with all his ancient pride, resolved never to give in and never to approve. It was the officer in him; he had lived in a class above and apart, almost in another world" (p. 114). But Moriya himself has in the past lived literally, and now lives emotionally apart, "in another world," and he has already confessed to his own self-cultivated "inability to feel." Thus, when he thinks of the Ueno subway crowded with homeless war victims, he muses: "But, Ushigi, . . . you have no time to think of that. You just live within yourself, convinced that your life is over." And again the accusation falls as much upon him as upon the ex-admiral. At times, Moriya is almost aware of the truth. Near the end of the novel, in another important meeting—with his daughter, Tomoko—Moriya compares himself with Ushigi. "Everyone lives in his own queer way," he says, "Ushigi, and I too. I don't suppose you understand yet, but we're like these lanterns. We hang dangling in this world, and there's something sad about us. But it's not that anyone else made us that way. It's ourselves, we ourselves. Honestly" (pp. 235–36). The reader can believe him.

The major themes by which Osaragi conveys the identity motif throughout the novel also appear in the Moriya-Ushigi meeting. When Moriya accuses Ushigi of "curling up inside his shell," the image of a small, confined space recalls the narrow prison cell where Moriya is first challenged as to his identity. Images and expressions of freedom and bondage occur throughout the book. The narrow cell, in fact, is like the Japan, the "narrow country" to which Moriya repeatedly refers.[5] Significantly, Moriya's references to the narrow land include the notion of bondage in terms of emotional involvement. "A man could not be alone in his daily life," he complains to himself when he meets Tomoko. "There were endless conflicts and compromises, but it was impossible to find a harmony within oneself alone. There were just too many people. This was a narrow land" (p. 254).

Again, in Kyoto, site of traditional Japanese culture, Moriya's ambiguous status is framed in terms of past and present. He is in bondage to neither, he claims. "He did not belong to the old Japan, nor was he one of those who were going to create something for the New Japan. He could see both worlds just because nothing bound him to either. And it was with the belief that nothing would bind him that Kyogo made his trips to Kyoto" (p. 213). But Moriya's kind of "freedom" is difficult to maintain, as he discovers. Under the spell of Kyoto, his desire to belong— weakness as he sees it—is transferred to an aesthetic form which he finds it possible to accept. "Kyogo never became sentimental. But he would sense an indescribable, delicate atmosphere enfolding his body, and feel, wonderfully deep down, that he had come back to Japan. He didn't mean to let anything bind him, but something like a mist or an ether was stealing into his heart insensibly and satisfying his longing for the old Japan" (p. 215). He thus sublimates his emotional hunger into a vague, misty longing. Ironically, his emotional emptiness has its symbolic counterpart in the cramped old Kyoto houses, "with their interiors invisible from the street, with hardly any exposure to the sunlight." Like the Kyoto poor, who he says have fashioned for themselves a world of "melancholy and unfulfillment," he adopts an aesthetic of loneliness (pp. 211–12).

Related to the freedom-bondage theme are those of life-death and Europe-Japan. Moriya's challenge to Ushigi— "You've killed in this mad war, even your son you've killed, and you're still alive yourself. It's half a miracle that you're alive. Don't you want to make something of that life?" (p. 112)—is echoed by the artist Onozaki, later. "That's how we are," he says to Moriya's daughter, "the perfect citizens for a dead nation. . . . It's no easy thing to live" (p. 170). The young and vigorous Yukichi and Tomoko, representative of Japan's hope for the future, are both described as "alive" (pp. 122, 131). Moriya, however, admits to being a "corpse," and in his confrontation with Professor Oki says that he might "infect those who come too near" (p. 277). Clearly, to be alive is to be involved. Osaragi adds the ironic note of Moriya's "official death": "The dead shouldn't disturb the living," Moriya says to Tomoko when they meet. "You know something? The name of Kyogo Moriya has been erased from Japan's census register. He's dead. By law, a missing person is considered dead." Tomoko joins in the half-jest, saying, "There is your grave, Father." Ironically, Moriya has never been closer to "life"—real emotional involvement —than in his meeting with the vital Tomoko (p. 237).

Numerous comparisons between Europe and Japan add depth to the identity theme. The two "worlds" are extensions of Moriya's divided self, and frequent references keep the reader aware of his ambivalence. When he is with Ushigi, he remembers how different the cathedral carillons sound from Japanese bells (p. 110); in Kyoto, the temples have "nothing alive" in them, while Moriya remembers the cathedrals of France and Italy as having been "still filled with the life of the people" (p. 207). But the relationship between country and emotional involvement is made explicit in terms of what Moriya regards as weakness. Confident his long life abroad has made him "too strong for any human being to weaken him," he yet admits to having "become weak since I came back to Japan."

> And that seemed to be the truth. The intense consciousness of solitude that had given him his strength while living abroad had been growing thinner and thinner here in Japan. He seemed to be fusing somehow with the people he came into contact with, indeed even with the scenery he saw. . . . And those strangers' lives would mingle with his somehow, so that he seemed to know the sufferings and joys of their daily lives and understand the minutest motions of their hearts. He had never felt like that in his walks over the stone-paved streets of Europe. But he was on the soil of Japan now, really, he could not help but know it. He meant to stand alone, but something was moving in the blood with which he had been born, something compelling stirred in the unknowable recesses of his soul. . . . Europeans lived behind thick walls, and could be indifferent to their neighbors, but in Japan only thin paper panels and bamboo fences separated one from the street outside. There were no barriers. A man could not be alone in his daily life. (pp. 253–54)

Osaragi doesn't explain what sufferings, joys, or other feelings Moriya might experience here, and the result is another vague, almost mystical ("something compelling . . . soul") sublimation of his need to belong. And again the irony is apparent; for Moriya, "strength" is withdrawal; "weakness" is warm, human involvement. "I'd feel more at home in a foreign city," he confesses to Ushigi near the end of the book. "There's always someone in my way here, wherever I go" (p. 286).

The "someone" in his way in the book's final scene is Saeko Takano, and Moriya avoids any involvement by leaving her and Japan. Earlier, he has given a surface explanation of the problem to Ushigi. "Most of us have no solid roots in the ground," he says. "That's the basic problem. Aimless movement, yes indeed, everything here is just that. The rootless plant blows as the wind lists" (p. 288). Aimless movement is of course characteristic of Moriya, and his restlessness is typical of one feature of mid-twentieth-century man. Anthropologist Masao Yamaguchi, commenting on the restlessness manifested by student rioting throughout the world, attributes much of the underlying discontent to the "lack of a spiritual center."[6] For a given individual, the "center"—broadly interpreted—may consist of any number of different things. But Osaragi's protagonist lacks or rejects family, place, community, vocation, class status, religion, political allegiance, and "success" of some kind—in short, all of the traditional roots which give rise to a healthy self-image.

Thus beneath Moriya's restlessness and failure to identify is his failure at self-acceptance and interpersonal involvement. With his usual mixture of half-truths, Moriya says to his daughter, Tomoko, "I confess I'm an egotist and a wanderer. I've trained myself to live without feeling too much sadness or loneliness. . . . What's more, living in this world is not a matter of trying to iron out your relationships with others; to the end it is a matter of struggling with yourself. I'm a man who has calmly deserted his wife and child; a heartless egotist; an old man who's already become indifferent to human emotions" (p. 236). Among the truths of his statement is his admission of self-struggle. Since he lacks the self-acceptance which leads to satisfying relationships with others, his life is indeed a self-struggle, something Western theologians long ago labeled *incurvatus se*, a turning inward upon oneself. This incurvature is dramatized in the story by Henri de Régnier that Moriya recalls near the end of the novel. A "very ordinary man" retires from his barren life and settles down to enjoy an acacia tree in his yard:

> It was a perfect friend. There were no complications in its friendship, as there might be with a human being; it just filled his quiet days with satisfaction. . . . In a little while the acacia, old like himself, had become his dearest friend, and he had begun to feel that their lives were bound up together somehow, his and his tree's. A very natural feeling for a lonely old man to have.
>
> One morning, while he was still in bed he heard an unusual sound outside. He jumped up and rushed to the window. Some laborers had been sent from the city hall. They were at his acacia. They had lopped

off the branches already, and were starting to fell the naked trunk. The acacia was a hindrance to traffic, standing where it did, and it had to be removed. (pp. 267–68)

The story serves as a parable of Moriya's self-pity and self-involvement, revealing his unhealthy fixation. Like the acacia tree in the story, and the now-useless castle moat which reminds him of the story, Moriya too will have to be removed.

In terms of the popular psychoanalytic "games analysis," Moriya's pastime might be labeled "I'm Destined to Suffer" (IDS).[7] "I came back to Japan homesick for my fatherland," he tells Saeko; "as it's turned out, I might as well have been a tourist here for the first time. A lonely thing, but that doesn't matter to a man like me" (p.295). Here his internal Child seeks emotional comfort. Sometimes his internal Parent responds, sometimes other parental figures (Ushigi, Oki). A "games analysis" of the advantages gained by Moriya's emotional strategy might go as follows: (I) Internal Psychological—compensation for guilt, (2) External Psychological—avoidance of responsibility, (3) Internal Social—I'm destined to suffer, (4) External Social—I'm a noble martyr, (5) Biological—masochistic, (6) Existential—I am helpless (blameless).

Moriya's psychological game ends with a game. Structurally, the novel is framed by two gambling scenes, one near the beginning where Moriya's skill-luck is demonstrated, and the wager with Saeko at the end. In psychological gamesmanship the one who successfully lures his opponent into a "game" is bound to win. Moriya is leaving; he "wins" (avoids emotional involvement) no matter whose card turns up. It is appropriate, however, when the queen of spades, his card, shows first. The card game is thus a kind of ritual enactment of the psychological game Moriya has already won.

Thus Osaragi over-romanticizes his hero, and the result is almost one of those postwar gentlemen "who can neither destroy nor create," as the artist Onozaki describes them. The artist's terms are suggestive, and one is tempted to conjecture that in Moriya's problem of identity there is just a hint of the artist's. At least Moriya's struggle with involvement and detachment is a struggle with the same twin bugaboos which have long plagued the artist. Perhaps the all too "popular" Osaragi reflects through his hero (consciously or unconsciously) what might be his own deepest concern, the integrity of his art. Moriya frequently raises the question of commitment to action, but refuses to "live" himself. At one point the artist Onozaki says, "I'm going to put the misery of men on canvas . . . and the pain they have in living. . . . Of course, my paintings aren't pretty. . . . They won't sell" (pp. 87–88). Perhaps he speaks here for Osaragi.

In any event, *Homecoming* is not a banal "pop" version of postwar Japan. It is not without flaws: it is structurally weak, an art theme is suggested but left undeveloped, and some minor incidents detract from rather than add to the central idea. But the novel is an intriguing portrait of a modern man who, in an age when greater self-awareness develops a greater need for self-acceptance, fails ultimately to claim his humanity. It is only too easy to identify with Moriya, for he is an appealing embodiment of an all-too-familiar pattern. His words near the end of the novel linger disturbingly: "It's lonely being by yourself there, that's true enough, but you *can* be by yourself, wherever you go. Life was less troublesome that way, the line between oneself and others was so clearly drawn" (p. 288).

5

THE CREATIVE QUEST

Life is an art, something which the hero of *Homecoming* never fully realizes. At its fullest, it is a person's potential realized in creative freedom. For someone whose attempts to reach such an ideal are distorted or strangled by inhibitions, the quest may be a traumatic struggle. It may culminate in a dramatic act symbolic of the personality's urge toward creative expression and wholeness. In *The Temple of the Golden Pavilion*, Yukio Mishima probes the troubled world of his psychologically disturbed young protagonist, portraying not only the quest for identity, but at the same time suggesting a parable of the artist for whom the Ideal is—just as it is for young Mizoguchi—at once inspiration and terror, a beckoning goddess and an inhibiting threat.[1] The book's modernity, if not its uniqueness, lies in this.

Actually, Mishima's novel is both traditional and modern. It is traditional in that the protagonist is a Buddhist acolyte and the action occurs in and around a temple (Kinkakuji) and a city (Kyoto) famous as symbols of traditional Japan. There are numerous references to Zen rituals, and certain famous Zen *koan,* or parabolic riddles, appear during the narrative. It is modern, however, in its psychological probing and use of abnormal behavior, especially sexual aberration. It is especially twentieth century in its subtle linking of the trials of the protagonist with the trials of the artist.

The story thus has at least three levels of interest. Historically, it draws on the event which both dismayed and intrigued the Japanese, the burning of the famous Golden Pavilion, Kinkaku, of Kyoto's Rokuon Temple in 1950 (since restored) by a Zen Buddhist acolyte. The Golden Pavilion, completed perhaps about 1398, had become a National Treasure, symbol of the beauty, richness, and imperishability of Japan's cultural heritage. At the trial, the acolyte testified to a consuming self-hatred and a hatred of anything beautiful. A psychiatrist diagnosed the young man as a "psychopath of the schizoid type."[2] The narrative gains a certain strength from the perennial appeal of the story behind the story, the human drama behind the headline. It shares in this respect with numerous other works based on or around such events as the Sacco-Vanzetti trial, the Haymarket riots, and, most notably, the countless novels drawing upon wartime incidents. *Black Rain* is an obvious example. In the case of the Golden Pavilion, a monument invested with so much cultural pride would be well calculated to arouse interest.[3]

On the fictional story level, the event becomes an intriguing imaginative recreation of a disturbed ego striving to achieve liberation from the repressive forces which threaten it. It is again a quest for identity, this time not the soldier's traumatic ordeal, nor the sentimental ex-patriate's, nor the existential trapped hero's, nor the shrinking old man's, but the suffering youth's struggle to grow and comprehend relationahips which at the same time tempt and terrorize. "Which personality is really lasting?" the troubled protagonist asks. "The one that I envisage myself or the one that other people believe I have?" (p. 246). Among modern Japanese writers, no one except Kobo Abe has been so preoccupied, one might even say obsessed, with the identity theme as Mishima. *Confessions of a Mask, Forbidden Colors,* and, in a bizarre way, *The Sailor Who Fell from Grace with the Sea* also develop the theme of a troubled, sexually confused young man's search for self-understanding.[4] In *The Temple of the Golden Pavilion,* the quest climaxes when the young acolyte, Mizoguchi, sets fire to the temple in which he is supposed to serve out his lifetime. When he tries to mentally prepare himself for the act by first visiting the gay quarters to lose his virginity, he again reveals the identity confusion which plagues him. "How could I have convinced myself of the idea that the I who was contained in those clothes would be an entirely different person?" (p. 220).

Mizoguchi's act is creative as well as destructive. Clearly, the burning of the temple is liberating, and Mishima significantly retains a kernel of the original here. His fictional protagonist, like the young acolyte who burned the real Golden Pavilion, does not regret the deed. In fact, whatever shame, guilt, terror, or other feeling that may have prompted the original's suicide attempt is played down in Mishima's work. At the novel's end, though he has brought a bottle of arsenic and a knife with him, Mizoguchi simply throws them down a ravine, takes out a cigarette, and begins to smoke. "I felt like a man who settles down for a smoke after finishing a job of work," he recalls. "I wanted to live" (p. 262). He feels free. He has reached a new stage in his growth toward creative freedom.

The temple is a complex symbol, indeed so complex that one critic views the entire novel as a kind of Zen *koan* in which the temple is "beautiful and ambiguous" and yet "creates contradiction, opposition, and discord." Presumably, the temple is as tantalizing and evasive as life itself.[5] But the complexity is at least partly understandable in terms of psychological dynamics which account for some of Mizoguchi's ambivalence as well as some of the temple's ambiguity. Among the young acolyte's psychological "hang-ups," one of the most obvious is his sexual frustration, indicated by his failure to consummate the sex act with a woman until just before he burns down the temple. Fire has always been a powerful symbol of sexuality. People speak of the "flame of love" and "fire of passion"; men and women who are sexually excited, or excitable, are said to be "on fire" or "hot." To "play with fire" is to indulge in a dangerous or forbidden affair. One who is jealous is "burned up." A former lover is an "old flame." All such euphemistic terms, some psychologists say, grow from an unconscious acceptance of the erotic symbolism of fire.[6] Shortly before he burns the temple, Mizoguchi observes an old sign at the entrance to the pavilion dining room:

A–TA–KO HOLY SIGN
Beware of Fire

"I wonder whether I shall be believed when I say that during these days the vision of fire inspired me with nothing
less than carnal lust," Mizoguchi reflects (p. 220). Once
again the reader can believe.

The trouble stems in part from a traumatic experience
he has as a junior high school age boy when he returns
home for summer vacation. He becomes aware of what
turns out to be his mother's adulterous act with a distant
relative when he notices the mosquito net of the bed moving in an odd manner. He and his father and mother and
the relative are all sleeping together. When Mizoguchi
turns to observe the source of the movement he is shocked
by the sight and feels "as though a gimlet was drilling
into the very center" of his eyeballs. His father suddenly
notices, covers the boy's eyes with his hands, and thus
cuts off the "terrifying world" and buries it in darkness
(p. 55). The effect of this oppressive event is intensified by
another, a rudimentary encounter with a girl, Uiko, who
is one of his adolescent sex fantasy objects. When he im-
pulsively jumps out into the road before her bicycle early
one morning, he experiences a humiliating rejection
which is like being "turned into stone." He describes his
frustration as the loss of contact between the "outer
world" and his own "inner world," and again speaks in
terms of identity: "The 'I' who had slipped out of his uncle's house, put on white gym shoes and run along this
path through the darkness of the dawn until reaching the
keyaki tree—that 'I' had made merely its inner self run

hither at full speed. . . . Something had bestowed reality on all this without waiting for my participation" (p. 11). Uiko's reaction almost paralyzes Mizoguchi with shame. "Good heavens!" she says. "What an extraordinary thing to do. And you only a stutterer!" (p. 12).

His sexual confusion is directly associated with the temple. On several occasions a vision of the temple prevents him from the sex act. One is an incident at Kameyama Park. Mizoguchi, his friend Kashiwagi, and two girls go on a picnic. Later, alone with his date, Mizoguchi slips his hand under her skirt but is interrupted by an odd vision: "Yes, the Golden Temple appeared before me—that strange building which, when one thought it was near, became distant, that building which always floated clearly in some inscrutable point of space, intimate with the beholder, yet utterly remote!" He hesitates; the girl senses his timidity and turns her back to him in scorn (pp. 125–26). Again later, Mizoguchi confronts a discarded lover of Kashiwagi's, the woman whom Mizoguchi had observed three years before offering her breast to an army officer. She now offers her breast to Mizoguchi, but again a vision intervenes. "The Golden Temple once more appeared before me. Or rather, I should say that the breast was transformed into the Golden Temple." He is forced to endure a "cold, scornful look" (pp. 152–53).

Mizoguchi also associates the temple with his father, particularly in what he repeatedly refers to as its function of "cutting him off from life." The emphasis begins with the book's opening sentence, "Ever since my childhood, Father had often spoken to me about the Golden Temple" (p. 3). Mizoguchi's image of the temple is derivative; it is the image his father conveys to him. "Though occasionally I saw the real Golden Temple in photographs or in textbooks, it was the image of the Golden Temple as Father had described it to me that dominated my heart. Father had never told me that the real Golden Temple was shining in gold, or anything of the sort; yet, according to Father, there was nothing on this earth so beautiful as the Golden Temple" (p. 4). After his father's death, Mizoguchi talks with a young friend, Tsurukawa, who says, "The reason you like the Golden Temple so much is that it reminds you of your father." Mizoguchi records that this is "half-correct reasoning" (p. 39). But only half. For his attitude toward the temple-father relationship has a dark side. When he first visits the temple his father is seriously ill, and the journey is a sad one. His father's world is a "world of death," he thinks, and he feels that the ancient, sooty train is "headed for the station of death" (pp. 22–23). The dirt and soot make his consumptive father cough; twice the old man lays his "emaciated hands" on the boy's shoulders. The second time, they appear to change. "When I glanced at my shoulder," Mizoguchi records, "I saw that in the moonlight Father's hand had turned into that of a skeleton" (p. 29).

The father's hands provide a symbolic key to the complex associative function of the temple. They foreshadow Mizoguchi's record of the occasion when they close him off from the sight of his mother's adultery (which of course takes place earlier in Mizoguchi's life):

The memory of those hands is still alive within me. Incomparably large hands. Hands that had been put

round me from behind, blotting out in one second
the sight of that hell which I had seen. Hands from
another world. Whether it was from love or com-
passion or shame, I do not know; but those hands
had instantaneously cut off the terrifying world with
which I was confronted and had buried it in darkness.
(p. 55)

Mizoguchi's mind forges from his experience an associative train whose links are father, hands, temple, sex, and
being "cut off from life." He says that after his father's
death he was "freed from the fetters of his hands" (p. 56),
but as his own record shows, he is not. Instead, he transfers the inhibiting power of those hands to the Golden
Temple. Thus, when Kashiwagi attempts to seduce a girl
by first feigning an injury to win her sympathy, the nervous Mizoguchi hurries to the temple for relief. "This
temple, by just standing there as it did, was a controlling
force, a regulating force," he says. "Beauty such as this
could cut me off from life and protect me from life" (p.
111). When he tells of failing with the girl at Kameyama
Park, he says that the temple "came and stood between
me and the life at which I was aiming" (p. 125). When he
fails with the woman who offers him her breast, he asks,
"Why does the Golden Temple try to protect me? Why
does it try to separate me from life without my asking it?"
(p. 153). Of several other sexual opportunities, he says,
"Between the girl and myself, between life and myself,
there invariably appeared the Golden Temple" (p. 157).
His primary feeling is resentment; though he acknowledges the temple's "protective" function, he feels most

keenly its prison-like quality of barring him from "life."

His ambivalence toward the temple is intensified by his relationship with the Superior of the temple, Father Dosen. Mizoguchi alternates between desire for acceptance from the priest and puzzled resentment of his soft, pink flesh and sensual indulgence. He envisions melodramatically a moment with the Superior "when two human beings come to understand each other" (p. 168). At other times he thinks of the priest as a "nonentity." Mizoguchi tries desperately to gain attention from this father-surrogate; he is frustrated and bewildered by the man's silence. Near the end of the novel, his ambivalence crystalizes when he finds the Superior bowed to the floor in the Tower of the North Star. His feelings vacillate at first, then stiffen. "Although I was trying to reject it with all my strength, the fact was I was on the verge of succumbing to affection for him. But the thought that he had adopted this posture for my special benefit turned everything into reverse and made my heart even harder than it had been before" (p. 237). As Superior, and the one to whom Mizoguchi's future is entrusted, the priest is in the boy's mind inseparably connected with the temple.

But Mizoguchi's attitude toward the temple is still further complicated in that he regards it with mixed self-loathing and self-love. He is a stutterer, plagued by that outer manifestation of his inner frustration, and uglier than others, he feels. The temple is preeminently beautiful. "Even when I saw a beautiful face," he says, "the simile would spring into my mind: 'lovely as the Golden Temple' " (p. 22). Longing to share the beauty, he finds a link in the thought that he and the temple share a common danger. "I was almost intoxicated with the thought that the fire which would destroy me would probably also destroy the Golden Temple. . . . Just like my own frail, ugly body, the temple's body, hard though it was, consisted of combustible carbon" (p. 46). Later, he almost accomplishes a mental fusion which he describes as entering "that vision" which had separated him from life that afternoon in Kameyama Park. "Did I possess the temple, or was I possessed by it? Or would it not be more correct to say that a strange balance had come into being at that moment, a balance which would allow me to be the Golden Temple and the Golden Temple to be me?" (p. 131). And yet he resents the temple, and when he projects his self-hatred onto it, it becomes an object to be destroyed, an enemy to be eliminated. There is much truth to his admission that his attachment to the temple is rooted in his own ugliness (p. 39). It applies both to his desire for and hatred of the object.

Thus the temple is many things to Mizoguchi. It is a complex embodiment of his ambivalence concerning beauty, his parents, and himself. It is an imposing phallic symbol, an object of envy and at the same time a threat the memory of which frustrates and inhibits his every attempt at sexual expression. Similarly, it is a constant reminder of his parents—father, father-surrogate, and mother too—who have chosen his life's work as minister to its beauty and whom he loves and needs, yet hates and resents for keeping him from "life." And it is an extension of himself, a wish-fulfillment image of the beauty that is not his, and a despised symbol of the self-hatred that he projects. Gradually, it becomes even more, till it assumes giant proportions as a symbol of all that frustrates and confuses, of all that he loves and hates, of all that demands expression but is locked up within. It is too much to bear.

Psychologists offer various explanations for pyromania. According to one it may be a fetish pattern of sexually aberrant behavior in which, typically, there is some early strong emotional association with fire which is sexually exciting.[7] Another sees defiance of authority, expression of hostility and aggression, and the attempt to resolve unconscious sexual conflict as its chief dynamics.[8] It is often an attack against that which curtails one's freedom, moral or sexual, says a third.[9] Most if not all of these factors apply to Mizoguchi's act. It is surely an attempt to resolve the conflict within him, in this case by eliminating that which has become a symbol of the conflict. Surely, too, it is aggressive, hostile, defiant, and destructive, an attempt to remove the inhibiting barriers which stifle him. And he has a strong emotional association with fire; he remembers the burning of his father's coffin, when the "flames stood out distinctly" and he heard the horrible sound of the coffin lid springing open (pp. 34-35). From another point of view, the burning of the temple is a creative act, liberating, an effort of his troubled psyche to free itself and establish a wholesome contact with the world he fears, yet needs. It is an attempt to create order out of chaos.

Mishima develops Mizoguchi's psychic quest through several interrelated themes. One is the freedom-bondage motif.[10] Perhaps the initial image here is the "given" habit of stuttering, that physiological sign of psychological distress. It is an apt symbol of bondage, for the failure to communicate one's feelings is the failure to obtain release. Early in the novel, a naval engineering student returns to his old junior high school, triumphant in his fine uniform. When he suddenly calls, "Hey, Mizoguchi!" and gets only a stare, he wonders why. One of the students, anxious to impress, answers instead of Mizoguchi. " 'I'm a st-st-stutterer,' replied one of his admirers in my stead, and they all doubled up with laughter!" Mizoguchi retaliates by secretly carving ugly marks on the engineering student's beautiful black scabbard, an act which adumbrates his later firing of the temple (pp. 7–9). His life at the temple is also a bondage, both in terms of its dreary routine, separated from ordinary life, and as the preparation for the life-long service to which he has been bound by his parents. He describes spending one year "like a bird trapped in a cage" (p. 45). When he hears of Japan's defeat, and realizes the Golden Temple will not be destroyed by bombs, he nearly despairs. "I could hear this eternity," he laments, "which was like a curse on my head, which had shut me up in the golden plaster" (p. 64). This "curse" in turn harks back to an earlier bondage, when his father's hands had covered his eyes, protecting him, yet shutting him out from life.

Mizoguchi stresses the positive side of the freedom-bondage theme as he gradually resolves to burn the temple. For the first time, his acolyte's life becomes bearable. "I even forgot my hatred for the Superior! I had become free—free of my mother, free of my companions, free of everything" (p. 201). Actually, the Superior remains as a barrier in his mind. But when he later sees the priest crouched in the tower, he hardens his heart

[86]

and feels as if they had come to inhabit different worlds. The feeling acts as a release. "I was free from all trammels," he says (p. 237). Ironically, it is one of the Buddhist *koans* which overcomes the last of his reticence. He ponders the famous directive: "When ye meet the Buddha, kill the Buddha! . . . When ye meet your father and mother, kill your father and mother! . . . Only thus will ye attain deliverance. Only thus will ye escape the trammels of material things and become free." These words, he says, "propelled me out of the impotence into which I had fallen" (p. 258). His metaphor is significant. One of the most liberating experiences has been his encounter with a gay quarters prostitute with whom he loses his virginity. This girl, he claims, had looked at him with a look one might give to "some fellow human being." To his surprise, his existence is affirmed. "I was being handled like a man who is part of a universal unit. . . . After I had taken off my clothes, many more layers were taken off me—my stuttering was taken off and also my ugliness and my poverty" (pp. 224, 228). The frustrated young man is almost ready to enter what he so frequently refers to as "life."

Mizoguchi's troubled search for freedom is also expressed in terms of the difference between his own inner world and the outer world from which he feels estranged. Again his stuttering is prominent. It is the first sound that he has difficulty uttering, he says. That first sound is "like a key to the door that separates my inner world from the world outside" (p. 5). He retreats inward, trying to find a source of pride in not being understood. "Those things which could be seen by others," he says, "were not ordained for me" (p. 9). Convinced that he is different from others, he imposes on the temple his own special vision, staking everything, he says, "not so much on the objective beauty of the temple itself as on my own power to imagine its beauty" (p. 19). The possibility of objective beauty in fact threatens him. "At the thought that beauty should already have come into this world unknown to me, I could not help feeling a certain uneasiness and irritation. If beauty really did exist there, it meant that my own existence was a thing estranged from beauty" (p. 21). Somehow, he senses how tenuous his link with reality really is. "I had a strangely dangerous feeling that the thoughts which existed within my head were kept in contact with the phenomena of the outer world by a single membrane of their sensitive, fragile skin" (p. 36). His friend, Tsurukawa, is a kind of interpreter, he says, who could translate his words into "the language of the real world" (p. 57). He gropes to express the confusion he felt while at university. "How shall I put it? I felt that the outside world was spotted and again that it was striped. My inner being and the outer world slowly and irregularly changed places" (p. 174). The temple is of course the barrier, the wall, the door that separates the two. Its burning will end the separation. "The rusty key that opened the door between the outer world and my inner world would turn smoothly in its lock. My world would be ventilated as the breeze blew freely between it and the outer world" (pp. 247–48).

Thus the quest of the young acolyte is for liberation, freedom, or what he calls "life." Though its culminating act is in part destructive, it is also in a profound way creative, the psyche's struggle for wholeness, self-expression, "identity." In the broadest sense, it is the art of life that Mizoguchi pursues; and his dilemma, struggles, and quest in a number of ways reflect those of the artist who, like the young protagonist, must find the words (or form) which will connect the inner vision with the outer reality, which will affirm and document its validity or give it a viable shape. From this point of view, the novel can be read as a parable of the artist, and one is tempted, after James Joyce, to think of it as a "portrait of the artist as a young schizophrenic," a label which, however facetious at first glance, may prove to be wholly other. For, as certain anthropologists and others have been proclaiming for some time, there may be, in the world of lunacy, a redeeming fancy of which we know all too little.[11] Research into the relationship between abnormal behavior and creativity is still like the first clumsy attempts to orbit a satellite; a universe lies beyond.

Harry Levin, writing about Joyce, comments that twentieth-century artists had no place to turn but inward, and the preoccupation with art and the artist is a result.[12] Mishima, at any rate, substantiates the claim, for the art theme is couched just below the surface in several of his works, implicit if not explicit. In *Forbidden Colors,* it surfaces strikingly in a passage that makes exciting commentary on *The Temple of the Golden Pavilion.* Yuichi, like young Mizoguchi, is involved in a conflict of worlds.

Would he and reality someday meet? In the place where he and reality might come together, not only would these harbingers of his desire already in exis-

tence eat away at reality, reality itself would eternally
bring forth fictional forms dictated by his desire. . . .
Was not this, however, the epitome of art, the very
model of the reality of artistic creation? In order for
Yuichi's desire to come into reality, either his desire
or his concept of what was real must perish. In this
world it is believed art and reality live quietly side
by side; but art must dare to break the laws of reality.
Why? In order that it alone may exist.[13]

For Mizoguchi, it is the Golden Temple that must perish,
that complex symbol, at once life-denying, creativity-
stifling, and yet inspiring, challenging, shining as ideal.
The form of the temple must give way that a new form,
the story of the temple, may exist. One almost forgets
that Mizoguchi narrates his own story, that the burning of
the temple is a release into creativity.

Critics have duly noted Mizoguchi's psychological
frustrations, but not his artist's eye. One can neglect the
latter only at the expense of a goodly portion of the novel,
for countless passages attest his sensitivity to shapes,
sounds, darkness, and light. Though he is unable to communicate his feelings to his new friend, Tsurukawa, his
inward eye is keen: "His white-shirted stomach rippled
with laughter. The rays of the sun that poured through
the swaying branches of the trees made me feel happy.
Like the young man's wrinkled shirt, my life was wrinkled. But, wrinkled as it was, how white his shirt shone
in the sunlight! Perhaps I too?" (p. 40). He later hears that
the girl he stepped on under orders of a drunken American
soldier has had a miscarriage, and the memory of the

event troubles him. "My deed had settled like gold dust within my memory and had begun to give off a glittering light that constantly pierced my eyes. The glitter of evil" (p. 86). In Kameyama Park, Mizoguchi is horrified to see Kashiwagi's girl friend kiss the cripple's club feet. "The entire composition of the park had lost its harmony," he says. "I felt that tiny cracks had begun to open up over all the surface of the picture in which we were contained" (p. 121). Innumerable references to darkness and light recall the terrifying moment when his father's hands buried him in darkness and he lay sleepless until morning came with its "dazzling light" (p. 55).

The art theme was incipient in Mishima's source, in the real-life acolyte who was obsessed with beauty. Mizoguchi, like his archetype, is haunted by the temple, its beauty a mysterious, troubling thing. "And beauty synthesized the struggles and the contradictions and the disharmonies in every part of this building—and, furthermore, it was beauty that ruled over them all! . . . Yet I did not know whether beauty was, on the one hand, identical with the Golden Temple itself or, on the other, consubstantial with the night of nothingness that surrounded the temple. Perhaps beauty was both these things. It was both the individual parts and the whole structure, both the Golden Temple and the night that wrapped itself about the Golden Temple" (p. 254). His confusion over beauty is an extension of the confusion within him, the chaos which he is subconsciously trying to reduce to order. The riddle of beauty is the riddle of the temple; the riddle of the temple is the riddle of his life. "I must make sure," he says before burning the temple, "that the terrifying concept of beauty, which makes people powerless to act, would not now intervene between me and my intention" (p. 224).

On the subconscious level, his intention to burn the temple is an attempt to reduce the chaos of his life to order. The order-chaos theme is another powerful ingredient in the novel's makeup. Throughout, Mizoguchi's thoughts are contradictory and confused, as he admits. But he is conscious of the appeal of form. The temple itself, he notes, had been "constructed by unrest," and its ostensibly uncoordinated design had "evolved naturally from the search for a style that would crystalize all the surrounding unrest" (p. 36). The novel's setting in the confusion of war and the immediate postwar era underscores the idea of chaos. Mizoguchi's recognition of his friend's skill at flower arranging thus hints of his own deepest wishes. "Nature's plants were brought vividly under the sway of an artificial order and made to conform to an established melody. The flowers and leaves, which had formerly existed *as they were,* had now been transformed into flowers and leaves *as they ought to be*" (p. 145). Is his final act then his own attempt at transformation? He records how as a youth he had entertained two opposing forms of power wishes. "On the one hand I enjoyed imagining how one by one I would wreck punishment on my teachers and schoolmates who daily tormented me; on the other hand, I fancied myself as a great artist, endowed with the clearest vision—a veritable sovereign of the inner world" (p. 6). Perhaps his goal is the transfiguration of those twin desires into one clear image. Perhaps too his meticulous attention to detail as he prepares to burn the temple is yet another hint of the order he so desperately covets. "I hope that people will recognize how carefully I went about everything," he says (p. 249).

And so he burns the temple. Its flames suggest something of the creative process. On its positive side, as elusive ideal, as reflection of that inner perfection of form which struggles to be born, the temple may have to perish in the process. As any would-be artist can testify, what is conceived in beauty may end in stillbirth; the execution may deride the original vision, reducing it to ashes. Yet create one must, or remain sterile. And on its negative side, as inhibiting threat, the temple must also be overcome, or the artist again reduced, like Mizoguchi, to impotence. In any case, the effort must be made, the creative drive for order and wholeness undertaken. For the artist, the ability to communicate his inward vision, to break, in the novel's terms, the barrier between the inner and outer worlds, is to give shape to the shapeless, to articulate the formless and dark. Skilled physicians of body and spirit know that health can indeed be an art. After he burns the temple, Mizoguchi creates his story, a compelling narrative, without stuttering. At the end of his quest he finds the words.

6

THE LAST EXTREMITY

In his Nobel prize acceptance speech, Yasunari Kawabata refers to his essay "Eyes in Their Last Extremity."[1] The title comes from the suicide note of the famous short story writer Ryunosuke Akutagawa (1892–1927). As his remarks show, Kawabata pondered the question of suicide and rejected it, for a time at least, as an unenlightened act. But the phrase which so struck him, "eyes in their last extremity," is incarnate in the person of old Eguchi, protagonist of *House of the Sleeping Beauties*.[2] In this novel, Kawabata poignantly explores the intimate thoughts of an old man, probing back to the source of his existence. In his sensual yearnings, erotic fancies, and subtle attempts at self-deception, Eguchi searches for the meaning of his life.

Like *The Temple of the Golden Pavilion*, Kawabata's work is at once traditional, from one called the most Japanese of writers, and modern—as modern as geriatrics, senior citizens, and Sunset Villages. The traditional side is apt to puzzle Western readers, who may well wonder what sort of guide rails one can grasp hold of when crossing this "spiritual bridge spanning between East and West," as the Nobel prize citation described the novelist.[3] The something Japanese about Kawabata is a meditative, sympathetic, sometimes wistful, and highly evocative understanding of nature, or rather, of the subtle interplay between nature and human existence. It has deep roots in the heritage from Japan's past, both religious and literary, from Buddhist reflection and Shinto mystique as well as their artistic calling card, the haiku poem. Thus, in *House of the Sleeping Beauties*, the wrist of one of the sleeping girls brushes over old Eguchi's eye and the scent brings "rich new fantasies." The old man's thoughts are like a poem: "Just at this time of year, two or three winter peonies blooming in the warm sun, under the high stone fence of an old temple in Yamato" (p. 48). The flowers in turn suggest old Eguchi's daughters. This passage, and others like it, illustrate what one critic has described as the "painfully delicate nuances and almost immeasurable subtlety peculiar to Japanese art and literature."[4]

But even for Japanese readers the Nobel prize winner's works sometimes appear strange and even uninviting. Is it because Kawabata's sad, fragmented world is also a world of resignation, of quiescent Buddhism? Is the voice of this most Japanese of Japanese authors the voice of the past? And if so, is his famous Nobel speech the swan-song of an age? Kawabata's translator, Edward Seidensticker, asked these and other questions in an address given in Tokyo in April 1968.[5] Commenting that Kawabata's great theme was loneliness, the impossibility of love—in short, alienation—Professor Seidensticker asked: why then is Kawabata neglected by a generation of young people that so visibly demonstrates its feeling of alienation? The answers are not easy to obtain. Nor is it entirely clear that the current young generation does in fact neglect its Nobel winner.[6] In any case, however "traditionally Japanese," however much "of the past," and however puzzling, Kawabata's artistry undoubtedly has much which declares its timelessness and relevance for the present.

What indeed could be more relevant—to any age—than loneliness, the hopelessness of love, alienation? From the frustrated lovers of *Snow Country* to the dreamily desiring man in "One Arm," Kawabata brilliantly evokes the poignancy of thwarted love.[7] His other major themes too are universally appealing. The "darkness and wasted beauty" which "run like a ground bass through his major work,"[8] represent an integral part of the heritage of both East and West. Old age and death too preoccupy Kawabata. He said after World War II that he would write only elegies, and in keeping with the resolve wrote such works as *The Sound of the Mountain* and *Thousand Cranes*.[9] *House of the Sleeping Beauties* can be added. Puzzling, then, he may be, in great part no doubt due to his poetic, elliptical style, but Kawabata is very relevant, "contemporary" in the sense that universal themes are always contemporary. And his major themes are all represented in *House of the Sleeping Beauties*.

Like Tanizaki's *The Diary of a Mad Old Man*,[10] Kawabata's work reveals the inner workings of an old man's mind, recording his efforts to make the erotic most of his last days. But Kawabata's novel has a sinister note, and the crimson velvet curtains of the sleeping beauties' room create a setting which might have come from one of the macabre works of Edgar Allan Poe. The sinister note is sustained, for death suffuses the narrative; from the opening pages where one reads that "the wind carried the sound of approaching winter" to the final lines where the dark girl's body is dragged downstairs, the reader suspects death. And death comes, as inevitably as it must soon come to old Eguchi. Kawabata's artistry manifests itself in the way he combines the suggestions of death with bits of setting, builds up suspense, and uses indirection to achieve a unified tone. The result would satisfy Poe's criterion for the ideal short story, one which has a "unique or single effect." The effect in this case is a feeling of inevitability, a gloomy sense that something is coming to an end, and that at the end death waits.

Thus Yukio Mishima spoke of *House of the Sleeping Beauties* as a work dominated by "strangling tightness" and likened it to "a submarine in which people are trapped and the air is gradually disappearing." The reader, he said, "knows with the greatest immediacy the terror of lust urged on by the approach of death."[11] Kawabata carefully cultivates this feeling of "tightness." The opening words of his story are a warning which at once suggest danger and a strange eroticism. Old Eguchi is "not to put his finger into the mouth of the sleeping girl, or try anything else of that sort" (p. 13). Kawabata quickly adds the sinister note. The house has a "secret," a locked gate, and when Eguchi arrives all is silent. The woman who admits him has a strange and "disquieting" bird design on her *obi* (kimono waistband). Images of death soon accumulate. The secret house is near the sea, and the sound of the waves is violent. "It was as if they were beating against a high cliff, and as if this little house were at its very edge. The wind carried the sound of approaching winter, perhaps because of the house itself, perhaps because of something in old Eguchi." The winter season and the nearby sea, both universal symbols of death, suggest the mood. Eguchi, before entering the room of the sleeping girl, recalls lines from a poetess who died young, "the night offers toads and black dogs and corpses of the drowned." He wonders if the sleeping girl will resemble a drowned corpse (p. 16).

Small wonder that old Eguchi begins this first visit to the secret house with "apprehension" and an "unpleasant emptiness." As the reader first suspects, then gradually realizes with deepening awareness, that "emptiness" is Eguchi's own. For the old man's series of visits to the house of the sleeping beauties is a series of confrontations with himself, a set of experiments in self-analysis in which his identity is very much at issue. What could force one to be more intensely introspective than a meeting at which the other person is only a presence, a body, and where one's musings, questions, charges are met only with silence or the slight movement of a hand? At such a time any "dialogue" is self-generated, self-sustained, and ultimately self-directed. And what, for an old man, could more intensify the confrontation than to have that other person be a kind of polarizing opposite, a soft, beautiful, and silent young woman? Such a meeting would heighten memories, call forth old sensations, and force a measurement of oneself in relation to their presence and the present moment.

Thus Eguchi begins his quest. Nearing seventy years of age, he feels that he is perched, like the secret house seems to be when the waves roar, on the edge of the cliff above the sea. Still clear of mind, and apparently still virile to some extent, Eguchi grows irritable at any suggestion that he might be senile or helpless like other old men who visit the house. "I'm all right," he growls at the woman of the house when she cautions him to be careful of the wet stones and tries to help him. "I'm not so old yet that I need to be led by the hand" (p. 71). But his vision is that of one in his last extremity. "An old man lives next door to death," he says in the final chapter (p. 81). What is it to be an old man, in one's last extremity? People in their thirties sometimes experience the first traumatic shudder in realization of time's fleetness. By the forties, horizons have constricted, doors have closed, the vocational crisis is reached. At fifty, the backward look begins, the crisis of identity becomes acute, depression sets in. And what of the old man, nearing the end? What hopes and pleasures remain? What self-deceptions lure him on? What does he hope to gain from the house of the sleeping beauties?

Kawabata divides his narrative rather formally, into five chapters. Unlike the familiar dramatic form, however, the final section is not a denouement; rather, the story builds to a climax which comes only in the last pages. In each of the first four chapters, Eguchi visits the secret house and spends the night, each time sleeping by the side of a different girl. In the fifth chapter, Eguchi's fifth visit, the old man finds that he has been allotted two girls. Before this last visit, Eguchi learns that one of the old men has died while staying in the secret house. For both Eguchi and the reader this fact, together with the discovery that there are to be two girls instead of one, heightens the suspense. In the night one of the girls dies, and at the end of the novel old Eguchi, shocked, stands gazing at the remaining beauty, wondering where they have taken the body of the other.

On his first visit the apprehensive Eguchi finds himself probing his past. As an older person often remembers, recreates, and sometimes writes "the story of his life" to forestall death and define his existence, so Eguchi relives events from earlier days. The imagined smell of baby's milk starts a series of associations. He first remembers a geisha lover's jealous anger over the baby milk she smelled on his coat. This in turn calls up the memory of a lover he had had before he married. He remembers a particular meeting when her breast had become lightly stained with blood. He next recalls the middle-aged woman who counseled him to count potential lovers as a means of getting to sleep. Soon his thoughts turn again to the girl "whose breast had been wet with blood," and he remembers especially the cleanness of her secret parts, and seeing her in in Kyoto in the midst of flowers and bamboo. When he takes one of the two sleeping pills provided, he dreams, first of embracing a woman with four legs, and next, that one of his daughters has borne a deformed child. The child is hacked to pieces in preparation for disposal. Horrified, Eguchi awakens to the four crimson walls. He takes the second pill and sleeps till morning. On this first visit, a number of images filter through Eguchi's mind and blend together; on subsequent visits they reappear, sometimes in altered form. Dreams and memories mix; erotic fancies and nostalgic reflections mingle to produce babies, blood, women's breasts and secret parts, and the women in Eguchi's life.

On his second visit two weeks later, Eguchi, somewhat more nervous than before, finds an even more beautiful girl awaiting him. Aroused by caressing her and by her "witchlike" beauty, he decides to violate the rules, discovers the girl is a virgin, and, surprised, resists the temptation. The girl's warm scent brings visions of flowers, and flowers recall memories of his three daughters. He especially remembers his youngest and how, when she had lost her virginity to a suitor, he had taken her on a trip to "revive her spirits," and they had seen a famous four-hundred-year-old camellia tree. In the camellia-like richness of the body next to him he feels "the current of life, the melody of life, the lure of life." Eguchi this time takes both sleeping tablets at once. His second visit has produced a melange of sensations akin to the first; the deep red of the girl's lipstick and the reflection of the crimson curtains on the girl's skin mingle with visions of the camellia and thoughts of virginity, women's breasts, mother, and sleep.

Eight days later, Eguchi makes his third visit to the secret house. Whereas the second girl was "experienced," the third is "still in training," the woman of the house informs him. The sight of the young girl and the two usual sleeping tablets causes Eguchi to ponder what it would be like to "sleep a sleep as of the dead." He then remembers a young married woman he had met at a nightclub and taken to his hotel three years before. "I slept as if I were dead," she had told him in the morning. His pleasure in hearing this "stayed with him like youthful music" (p. 62). Next, the sleeping beauty's open mouth and tongue recall a young prostitute Eguchi had disliked and dismissed one carnival night. He begins to ponder the problem of evil, recalls past sexual pleasures, and finally, embracing the sleeping girl, dozes and dreams of golden arrows and flowers. He awakens and rings in vain for the woman of the house; he wants to take some of the drug and sleep that deep, death-like sleep. The old man's thoughts have drifted from erotic fancies—the rounded shoulders, open mouth, and tongue—to thoughts of pregnancy, flowers, and, especially, sleep.

Before retiring on his fourth visit, Eguchi and the woman banter about death and "promiscuity," and, when he asks about "the worst one can get by with" in the house, the remarks turn to suicide and murder. When he lies beside the girl he feels that his successive visits have each brought "a new numbness" inside him (p. 74). The girl's strong scent reminds him again of the milky smell of a baby. He imagines a wild bird skimming the sea's waves, "something in its mouth dripping blood." Eguchi amuses himself with erotic play around the girl's face: "Taking the lower lip at its center he opened it slightly. Though not small in proportion to the size of her lips, her teeth were small all the same, and regularly ranged. He took away his hand. Her lips remained open. He could still see the tips of her teeth. He rubbed off some of the lipstick at his fingertips on the full earlobe, and the rest on the round neck. The scarcely visible smear of red was pleasant against the remarkably white skin" (p. 77). Eguchi closes his eyes, envisions a swarm of butterflies, and wonders if the bosom of the girl evoked the image. He leaves on her breasts "several marks the color of blood." In the morning he asks for, and is refused, extra sleeping medicine.

One can see in the structure of the narrative both progression and thematic unity. Eguchi's visits to the secret house follow the deepening season; autumn turns to winter and the fall rains become sleet and snow. The final visit is made in "dead winter." The suspense too deepens, as Eguchi's thoughts become increasingly serious and macabre. Part of the subtle buildup is the old man's gradually increasing desire for stronger medicine and the growing urge to join the sleeping beauties in their death-like sleep. Unity is achieved by the concentration on character—primarily old Eguchi—and on place, and by the continual piling up of sensuous imagery. Eguchi is in turn aroused, soothed, stimulated, troubled, and calmed by the touch, smell, and sight of the soft flesh beside him in the red room. Again, the recurrence of like or similar images also heighten unity; virginity, sexual experience, pregnancy, and babies vie or blend with thoughts of flowers, parts of a woman's body, blood, and the sleep of death. Like Nathaniel Hawthorne, Kawabata is especially deft in his use of color. The house of the sleeping beauties is a house of whites, reds, and blacks: the whiteness of skin and milk, the redness of velvet curtains and blood, the blackness of night, death, and thoughts of the dark sea.

Like Hawthorne, too, Kawabata symbolically probes

the human heart. Indeed the crimson-curtained room is both heart and womb. It is heart, where an old man living a death-in-life confronts his paradoxical opposite, a young woman who is life-in-death; here he relives his past loves and puzzles over his existence. Eguchi probes deeper and deeper into his consciousness or "heart" as he returns repeatedly to the secret house. And it is womb; in its warm comfort Eguchi's thoughts turn to baby's milk, pregnancy, sex, blood, and death. It is a feminine world, where the women of Eguchi's life parade through his dreams and reveries. Maternal in its appeal, the crimson room lures him ever deeper in thought and farther back in time, inevitably, to the first woman of his life, his mother, in whom the notions of babies and breasts, the hopes, fears, and anxieties, the sensations of blood and death have their source.

On a cold night in the dead of winter Eguchi makes his fifth visit to the secret house. An old man has died while sleeping beside one of the beauties, and references to that death dominate Eguchi's conversation with the woman of the house. Eguchi is startled to learn that this time there are two girls. In another Hawthorne-like touch, Kawabata makes one dark, the other fair. Eguchi turns to the dark girl first. Her lips remind him of a girl he had kissed forty years before, who had insistently denied having lipstick, despite the evidence produced by Eguchi's handkerchief. He next turns to the light girl and then, sandwiched between the two, takes one of the sleeping pills. As drowsiness overcomes him, his thoughts turn to the first woman of his life: "Now at sixty-seven, as he lay between two naked girls, a new truth came from deep inside him. Was it blasphemy, was it yearning? He opened his eyes and blinked, as if to drive away a nightmare. But the drug was working. He had a dull headache. Drowsily, he pursued the image of his mother; and then he sighed, and took two breasts, one of each of the girls, in the palms of his hands. A smooth one and an oily one. He closed his eyes" (p. 94). His mother had died when Eguchi was only seventeen. He recalls the grief and terror of that scene. " 'Yoshio. Yoshio.' His mother called out in little gasps. Eguchi understood, and stroked her tormented bosom. As he did so she vomited a large quantity of blood. It came bubbling from her nose. She stopped breathing. . . . 'Ah!' The curtains that walled the secret room seemed the color of blood. He closed his eyes tight, but that red would not disappear" (p. 95).

Thus Eguchi, an old man standing on the brink of senility-death, yearns to return to the source from which he first gained reason and life. In his "last extremity" he lies symbolically cradled within the protective covering of the two girls, and, clutching their breasts, journeys in thought to a time of security and warmth. In the blood-red room, the dark and light girls, their feet intertwined ("One of her feet was between the feet of the fair-skinned girl" pp. 92–93), encircle the old man like the yin and yang of totality, and he longs with incestuous longing to penetrate again to that comforting oneness, that matrix which is a mixture of life, hope, escape, and death. But his memory of mother is primarily a memory of suffering and death; the breasts that haunt his memory are withered, and no fresh milk will come from them. And so Eguchi dreams a succession of nightmares, erotic dreams of his honeymoon, of coming home to mother, and of blood-red flowers. He awakens to find the circle broken; the dark girl, of whom he had first murmured, "Life itself" (p. 86), is dead. Eguchi emerges from the warm, dreamy, illusory sleep to feel the cold press upon him for the first time. It is as if part of himself has died. He hears the callous remarks of the woman telling him, "Go on back to sleep. There is the other girl," and as the car takes the dark girl's body away, Eguchi stands shivering with extra sleeping medicine in his hand, gazing at the remaining fair beauty.

The reader who has come to identify with Eguchi will share something of the chilled numbness which characterizes the old man in the final scene. One has a sense of near paralysis, of having been reduced by events to a state of catatonic immobility. Perhaps it is this which prompts Mishima's submarine analogy. The suffocating or numbing effect again illustrates Kawabata's artistry. He achieves it by filling his short work with countless examples of paradoxical or contradictory thoughts, and the opposites of appearance and reality. They appear, sometimes several to a page, throughout the narrative. The result is tension, and for the reader, the feeling that he is pulled in different directions, none of them clear, or, as in Mishima's analogy, the feeling that one is trapped, immobilized by the certainty that death is inevitably approaching but that one can only remain fixed and gasp for air.

The contraries are apparent first in the nature of the story itself. Ugly old men sleep beside beautiful young girls; the young girls are alive, yet death-like in sleep. They are real persons, but the situation is artificial. The opposites of life and death, old age and youth, ugliness and beauty, reality and illusion continue throughout. Eguchi's thoughts expand these themes. On his first visit, he recalls that he has passed ugly nights with women. "The ugliness had to do not with the appearance of the women but with their tragedies, their warped lives" (p. 17). But he wonders if there is anything "uglier" than an old man lying beside a drugged girl. The woman's repeated admonitions about "rules" add further tension. Impotent old men might wish to but cannot violate the restrictions on behavior except in limited ways. Eguchi, however, can, but is caught between his own sense of integrity and the hopelessness of the situation even if he should "break the rules." Feeling the paradoxical strangeness of his visit, Eguchi complains inwardly that "not the smallest part of his existence" reaches the girl.

The tension of opposites increases on subsequent visits. Eguchi thinks he will not return to the secret house, but does. He feels guilty about his first visit, but acknowledges that "he had not in all his sixty-seven years spent another night so clean" (p. 35). He expects the same girl, but gets another, one whom the woman describes ironically as "more experienced." To Eguchi's protestations about "promiscuity," the woman mockingly refers to gentlemen she can "trust"—but then laughingly adds, "And what's wrong with being promiscuous?" (p. 38). Eguchi has thought that sleeping girls represented "ageless freedom" for old men; he now wonders if the secret house conceals the "longing of the sad old men for the unfinished dream, the regret for days lost without ever being had" (p. 39). When the girl talks in her sleep, Eguchi has a conversation which is not a conversation; he wonders if the guilt he feels is painful or if the secret feelings actually add to his pleasure. The ambiguity of his second visit is summed up as he muses upon how the girl could be "experienced"; his oxymoronic conclusion is that she is a "virgin prostitute" (p. 43).

On his third visit Eguchi hears that the girl, though sleeping, is somehow supposed to be "in training." The sight of the young girl's body saddens him and evokes a death wish; he longs for "a sleep like death," but hovers between this desire and the desire to stay awake for enjoyment. Aroused by the presence of the girl, he contemplates an "evil" deed, and then stops to consider what evil might really be, and what evil he might have done in his life. The girl, he imagines, might even be a kind of Buddha. His thoughts thus lead ironically to another contradiction: she is a temptation to evil, yet her "young skin and scent might be forgiveness" for sad old men. The contradictions continue through Eguchi's last visit, which begins with steaming tea to counteract the freezing cold. But now death dominates the atmosphere and the crimson curtains seem like blood. What has begun as a curious search for new pleasure and vitality has ended in death; the girl Eguchi calls "life" is dragged lifeless down the stairs of the secret house.

Thus Eguchi learns—for even an old man must learn—the brittleness of his existence, the subtlety of self-deceit. The young flesh beside him is real enough: real to the hand, the nose, the eye, the ear, the mouth; it is the illusion of youth that deceives. The thin-lipped woman of the house, like some ancient hag-guardian of the hell of self-delusion, mocks those who enter her domain. Her callous remarks and actions, like the artificial light which must remain on throughout Eguchi's nights in the crimson room, reveal the cold secrets of the house of sleeping beauties. For Eguchi, the safe warmth of the womb is no escape; the only "escape" is death itself. The comfortable oneness of things has been broken. In his last extremity he stands, a chilly old man asking questions of himself.

* * *

In *Diary of a Mad Old Man,* Junichiro Tanizaki's old man too stands on the brink. He is in fact seventy-seven, ten years older than Eguchi, Kawabata's protagonist. Like the latter, his thoughts focus on erotic pleasures, but unlike Eguchi, Tokusuke is impotent, unable to engage in sex other than when he occasionally gets to suck the toes of Satsuko or otherwise engage in the "necking" or "petting" which his beautiful daughter-in-law cleverly allows him. He records, quite candidly in his diary, his scheming for opportunities to be near Satsuko, as well as his fears and observations about his own health and approaching death. In contrast to Kawabata's lyrically symbolic eroticism, Tanizaki's is earthy, realistic, clinically detailed. The settings too contrast strongly. Eguchi's secret house is mysterious and isolated. Tokusuke is confined primarily to his own home or to brief excursions with his family.

Appropriately, the thrust of the novels is also different. The efforts of Tanizaki's old man are not so much a quest for identity as an attempt to preserve the image he understands well and more or less accepts. He tries to extract the last bit of life-juice from the shriveled facts of his existence, affirming through diary and desire the significance of who he is. For Tokusuke is aware that he is an old man, plagued with assorted physical ailments, apt to die any time, and that only a few things make life worth while (p. 8). His major preoccupations, actually, are three: his physical condition, his chances for erotic stimulation by association with Satsuko, and his diary record. His will to live focuses around this triumvirate. The latter two, sex and art, are twin manifestations of his creative zest for life. Both depend, alas, on the condition of his body, which is in a precarious state of being (Tanizaki here has a bit of fun with the tendency of some of his countrymen for hypochondriacal preoccupation). When he is excited by Satsuko, his blood pressure leaps. When he writes too long, he suffers fatigue. The spirit is willing but the flesh is weak.

But he is hardly crazy. The title's assertion, that he is a mad old man (*futen rojin*), is surely ironic. For one thing, his diary account is lucid. When he looks at the record of a year before, he realizes he is getting forgetful and acknowledges it. His analysis of his own motives is perceptive. Near the end of the novel, according to Nurse Sasaki, Satsuko complains that the old man's "peculiar mental condition" caused her to leave him at Kyoto with his nurse and come home by herself. She and her husband consult a psychiatrist who says that the old gentleman is "subject to what might be called abnormal sexual impulses" but that he is not really mentally ill. "It was just that he constantly needed to feel sexual desire, and in view of the fact that it helped to keep him alive you had to take that into account in your behavior toward him" (p. 163). And according to the old man's diary Satsuko's clever words and actions are apt to be suspect. She has managed at any rate to win from the old man an expensive beige purse, a three-million-yen cat's-eye jeweled ring, and, as the novel ends, a swimming pool. Moreover, the accounts of Nurse Sasaki and Mrs. Shiroyama seem to validate the old man's personal record.

But most of this is beside the point. The madness, rather, is the madness of life itself, the lunacy of a world where the creative drive is shackled to a decaying frame identified by pulsebeats, urine analysis, and doses of medicine—and described in complicated medical jargon. "8 January. Patient examined by Dr. K of the Urology Department. Reported hypertrophy of the prostate and microbial infection from anuria, and advised prostatic massage and antibiotics. Slight improvement in EKG. Blood pressure 143/65" (p. 172). Tokusuke himself has become over the years an expert in medicines, "enough to give a young doctor stiff competition," Dr. Katsumi admits (p. 169). The old man knows the relative merits of Dolosin, Nobulon, Adalin, Parotin, and countless others. Nurse Sasaki's careful enumeration of her instructions suggests the emphasis. "I was told to administer a 20 cc. injection of 20% glucose, with 100 mg. of vitamin B1 and 500 mg. of vitamin C, twice a day, morning and evening, as well as two tablets of Adalin and a quarter tablet of Solven half an hour before bedtime" (p. 166). Old Tokusuke's existence comes increasingly to be defined by such clinical facts of life. On the comic level—and there is a good deal of comedy—Tanizaki satirizes the Japanese in particular and modern man in general. On the more serious level, Tokusuke's fate suggests a society which has developed analysis of the physical functions to a remarkable degree, but shows myopia in comprehension of the spirit. I'm trying to put the *id* back in Yid, says the Jewish narrator in Philip Roth's *Portnoy's Complaint*. Tanizaki's mad old man only needs the bed restored to bedlam, a redress of the imbalance in a society in danger of dedicating itself to the quantitative instead of qualitative measure of man.

In his analysis of life-counseling cases in the *Yomiuri Shimbun*, Munesuke Mita cites the case of a Fukushima woman who describes a relatively comfortable and trouble-free life with one exception:

> But we all have one cross to bear: Father has a strange habit we cannot tell anybody about. He is absolutely faithful to Mother, but he has a passion for women's panties. The older he gets, the stronger his compulsion becomes. Mother and my oldest brother once tried to persuade Father, as patiently and considerately as possible, to give up doing such a thing; with his consent they then burnt about ten pairs of panties he had accumulated. However, they say Father was so upset afterwards that for two whole days he never said a word and didn't eat much either.[12]

In his sociopsychological analysis, Mita says that for this hardworking, industrious man, who neither drinks nor smokes and who never took a day off, an expression of long-repressed desires and frustrations is understandable. He is a man "who has lost all sense of autonomy in his work, who exists as one small cog in a huge machine, a single statistic in a bureaucratized organization."[13] Tokusuke's case is quite different, of course. Like Kawabata's Eguchi, he has led a sexually adventurous life, and has even contracted venereal disease in his youth. One can hardly call his life repressed. Yet he shares with the panty-obsessed man of the *Yomiuri* example in one thing: a protest against depersonalization and stifling of the life impulse. Though the body must inevitably decay, it is only half—and as the "mad old man's" vigorous spirit seems to testify, the less interesting half—of the human equation. As Tokusuke might see it, better than the march of medical progress are the lovely feet of Satsuko trampling on one's grave. Thus, when he protests that Tokyo is a rubbish heap, he rejects this symbol of modern, urban, technological life as a place unfit to be buried in. Real lunacy is the failure to recognize the creative, self-generative springs of one's existence. By this criterion, Tokusuke is the sane gauge against which society must be measured.

Tokusuke creatively affirms himself not only in his diary and his sexual fancies, but in the artistry by which he engages in the "game" both he and Satsuko understand, and of course by the skill with which he teases the reader to the same expectations he enjoys. "I was quick to make the most of this change to touch her bare feet. She stretched both legs out on the sofa and peeled off her nylons to show me. I put her feet on my lap and clasped each of her toes in my hand, one by one. 'They feel soft to me!' I said. 'You don't seem to have any calluses.'

'You're not looking hard enough! Try pressing over there'" (p. 20). Or again, when Satsuko lets him indulge in what she calls "necking" and then asks for three million yen ($8,400) for the cat's-eye jewel: "But this is serious. What'll we do if my wife sees it?" "Do you think I'd let that happen?" "Anyway, I can't afford it. You're being too hard on this old man!" "You look happy, all the same!" "I believe I *was* looking happy . . ." (p. 73). One expects the old man to die at the novel's end. In a sense he does. Forbidden even to write, he can no longer communicate his identity to the reader. But still he can fancy, as his son, Jokichi, seems to realize. "The old man's head is full of daydreams, just watching them work on that pool," he says. "And the children are looking forward to it too" (p. 177). The *Diary* is a happy book, and, as far as the reader knows, Tokusuke's last act is affirmative. There is in fact a touch of that archetypal figure, the Trickster, in Tanizaki's mad old man. One sees it in his mischievous delight in stirring up family friction, in his sexual urges, and most of all in his creative spirit which, one likes to think, transcends the inevitable. Erasmus would have liked Tokusuke; he would have seen in him an excellent likeness of his second class of "folly": "It is present whenever an amiable dotage of the mind at once frees the spirit from carking cares and anoints it with a complex delight."[14] The mad old man's identity is worth pondering.

7

IDENTITY FOUND

In *The Hard Journey,* Honor Matthews says that man's knowledge of himself is an irrational knowledge, and that the price to be paid for it is suffering.[1] As if to document the statement, Kobo Abe, in his Yomiuri prize-winning *The Woman in the Dunes,* has his hard-journeying protagonist suffer at length from sand, woman, and sinister sand-society in a Kafkaesque fantasy setting before finally coming to terms with himself and his environment.[2] Abe captured at least one of the moods of the postwar generation with this novel, and his protagonist resembles the self-probing, absurdity-confronting, identity-seeking heroes of Kafka, Sartre, Camus, and others in the West.

A comparison with Kafka is in fact a helpful starting point in coming to grips with this odd narrative. For one thing, the mixture of fact and fantasy, the juxtaposition of accurate detail and nightmare-like setting contribute the note of absurdity. After a mildly humorous and satiric opening chapter, the narrative begins. The entomologist-hero starts what appears to be an ordinary field trip after insect specimens. The descriptions are simple and realistic. "There were fields of potatoes and peanuts, and the odor of domestic animals mingled with that of the sea. A pile of broken shells formed a white mound at the side of the clay-and-sand road, which was as hard as cement" (p. 8). This innocent-appearing landscape soon becomes strange and, eventually, threatening. "The road alone rose, while the hamlet itself continued to remain level. No, it was not only the road; the areas between the buildings were rising at the same rate. . . . At length, all the houses seemed to be sunk into hollows scooped in the sand. . . . The slope suddenly steepened. It must have been at least sixty-five feet down to the tops of the houses. What in heaven's name could it be like to live there? he thought in amazement, peering down into one of the holes" (p. 9). He soon finds out, and thus, like Kafka's hero, Joseph K, in *The Trial,* he begins an ordinary day only to realize himself caught in some mysterious process, and subject to the whims of an equally mysterious "They."

In other ways too the work resembles Kafka's. The protagonist, trapped in an alien environment, spends his days trying to extricate himself. During his "trial" he undergoes a certain amount of introspective questioning, experiences guilt, and philosophically mulls over questions of time, death, and his relationship to existence. For example, at one point, musing over his plight, he feels as if he is observing himself. "Suddenly his eyes soared upward like a bird, and he felt as if he were looking down on himself. Certainly he must be the strangest of all . . . he who was musing on the strangeness of things here" (p. 160). Again, he ponders the strange beauty of the hostile sand which surrounds him: "What in heaven's name was the real essence of this beauty? Was it the precision of nature with its physical laws, or was it nature's mercilessness, ceaselessly resisting man's understanding?" (p. 182). About the passing of time he comments, "You like movies of wild animals and of war because you find that the same old day, following the same old yesterday, is waiting for you as soon as you come out of the movie house" (p. 183). In view of such metaphysical speculations, the comment that Abe "uses the techniques and tensions of science fiction to probe fundamental questions of alienation and identity" is true enough as far as it goes.[3] The same can be said of any number of modern works, however, and the comparison with Kafka, or any other writer, is at best of limited value. The solitary hero, trapped in a hostile environment, and puzzling over the nature of existence is indeed common, and any reader will undoubtedly recall from his reading background a number of features shared with Abe's novel. Abe's protagonist, for example, in some ways resembles the titular hero of William Golding's *Pincher Martin*. Both are threatened by a surrounding "sea" (cf. Abe's descriptions of the sand); both struggle to endure and cope with their hostile environment; both reflect on their past life and experience twinges of conscience concerning some "other woman." Such comparisons, if limited in usefulness, are nevertheless helpful in establishing the book's modernity and its relationship to other contemporary works of art.

For the critic, the trouble with such works (or virtue,

depending on the critic) is that they invite multiple inter-
pretations which, for the author, undoubtedly cause
chuckles of delight (or groans, depending on the author
and interpretation). Thus, *Woman in the Dunes* can be
read as a contemporary example, couched in a dream
setting, of the "I-novel" or biographical-confessional
narrative which has assumed such a long and important
role in the development of the modern Japanese novel. It
is worth keeping in mind, as Donald Keene suggests in a
study of Osamu Dazai, that much Japanese criticism is
apt to be biographical.[4] Such an approach might emphasize that Abe, like his protagonist, Jumpei Niki, was
born in 1924, and that as a young man he was interested
in insect-collecting. The story could be seen as a dramatization of his own intellectual and social development,
including his coming-of-age as an artist.[5] At one point
Niki engages in an imaginary self-dialogue concerning
art. He taunts himself: "Well, Niki, I am amazed. At last
you have decided to write something. It really was the
experience that made you. A common earthworm won't
attain full growth if it's not stimulated, they say" (p. 111).
Or the novel could be seen as Abe's own quest for identity, part of the continuing preoccupation shown in *The
Face of Another* and *The Ruined Map,* as well as in the
short story "The Wall."[6]

Freudian or other psychoanalytic critics might also find
the novel appealing. They would undoubtedly point out
the womb-like nature of the setting where the bulk of the
action occurs and note the protagonist's compulsive attempts to escape as well as the fact that he is safe from the
threatening villagers as long as he follows the sand-

woman's advice. They would note also Niki's sexual encounters with the woman, that he conceives a child with her, and that he ponders the nature of his previous sexual experience. Surely they would point to the bizarre dream Niki has in which a strange letter spurts blood when he presses it with his fingers (pp. 84–85). They might regard the fire tower which exercises surveillance over the sand-city area as a phallic image, and perhaps see in the three male villagers who regularly check on Niki's presence, withholding water when he fails to perform as expected, some kind of super-ego. The narrative in such a view would become a dream-fantasy in which the author explores the fears and obsessions of his hero (or himself).

One could also take a sociopolitical approach, combining the fact of Abe's one-time leftist leanings with certain suggestions in the novel to fashion a satiric critique of society in general and bourgeois culture in particular. The sand society thus becomes a symbol of arbitrary, meaningless, bureaucratic government whose demands and functions are enigmatic. The individual, trapped under these conditions, finds himself compelled to conform. Early in the narrative, Niki observes the house to be "already half dead," its insides "half eaten away by tentacles of ceaselessly flowing sand." He observes that "not a single thing could stand against this shapeless, destructive power" (p. 31). The corrosive power of the sand is here the corrosive power of bourgeois values, possessing and slowly destroying the human spirit. The motto of the village, "Love Your Home," becomes, in this view, a grim joke.

Any adequate interpretation must of course confront the work itself—its form, the outcome of the narrative, and such central features as the sand, the woman, and the trapped man. Western critics often charge Japanese novels with formlessness.[7] But though a fantasy setting might allow an author considerable freedom in this respect, Abe has endeavored to provide *The Woman in the Dunes* with a definite structure. In the opening chapter and the final legal notices about a missing person, he establishes a factual frame for the narrative. Chapter 1 notes that a man has disappeared, comments satirically on the reaction of police, people in general, and an amateur psychoanalyst to the disappearance, and concludes with the statement that since seven years have elapsed "without anyone knowing the truth," the man has been pronounced legally dead. Following the narrative, a "Notification of Missing Persons" and "Judgment" iterate the stiff, legal facts of the case. First impressions often linger. In a work of art they are usually intended to. It is impossible to determine to what extent the satiric and slightly ironic nature of the frame elements are meant to affect a reader. Nor can one legislate concerning reader reactions. The tone which the author establishes, however, is an important conditioner, and the nature and extent of one's involvement in a work usually depends on the tone he perceives. Kafka's *The Trial* is again a useful example. According to Max Brod, Kafka's friend and literary executor, friends of Kafka often broke up with laughter when he read aloud certain portions of his novel. An American college student reading *The Trial* in an English edition, however, is apt to become so engrossed with the frustrations and suffocating experiences of the hero that he fails to react to or even overlooks incidents of humor. But the satiric thrusts in *The Woman in the Dunes* are more obvious. Thus, after chuckling over the views of the "amateur psychoanalyst" of chapter 1—that "in a grown man enthusiasm for such a useless pastime as collecting insects was evidence of a mental quirk. Even in children, unusual preoccupation with insect collecting frequently indicates an Oedipus complex"—will a reader feel that "an almost unbearable suspense builds toward the final episode"?[8] Humor and suspense are certainly compatible; the one may indeed heighten the other. But the point is worth considering.

In any case, what takes place within the frame also has a structure. Abe divides his novel into three parts, a short opening section, a longer middle portion, and a very brief concluding part. The end of part 1 finds Niki frustrated and miserable. Discovering himself watched by three men from above, he shovels furiously at the sand of his "prison," only to collapse from nervous exhaustion and the heat. "Suddenly the flow of sand grew violent. There was a muffled sound and then a pressure against his chest. . . . He was only dimly aware of a faint milky light playing over him as he lay doubled up in the black splotch of his vomit" (p. 71). At the end of part 2 he has just failed in his attempt to escape but, though sorrowful, is able to philosophize: "There are all kinds of life, and sometimes the other side of the hill looks greener. What's hardest for me is not knowing what living like this will ever come to." Meanwhile, the sandwoman, speaking in a "soft, moving voice," prepares to wash him (p. 208). At the narrative's end, he finally possesses the means to escape, his "two-way ticket," but is "bursting with a desire to talk to someone about the water trap." He decides to stay and "put off his escape until sometime after that" (p. 239). Niki's lot obviously improves. In part 1 his actions are those of a frenzied, trapped animal. By the end of the book he has gained the freedom to decide "the destination and time of departure," but chooses to put off his escape indefinitely. Moreover, he has a purpose in remaining. He is excited about his water trap and wants to talk about it with the villagers.

Niki's adventures also have another kind of narrative form, for the overall pattern is that of a journey, or, more specifically, a quest. In this respect *The Woman in the Dunes* is another modern version of the familiar archetypal search motif. Perhaps a hint is supplied by the introductory frame chapter. Abe's hero *is* searching; he intends to collect insects that live in the dunes. What he discovers there is something quite different, however. Like Private Tamura, hero of *Fires on the Plain,* Jumpei Niki makes a metaphysical journey into the depths of his own consciousness. His physical journey is brief, from Tokyo to the fantasy land of the dunes. But once in the sand dwelling he confronts the exigencies of his existence. The deep sand-pit becomes another heart-of-hearts, a symbolic mental landscape where Niki faces the elemental facts of life: sand, woman, and himself. What is the outcome? Is the "quest" successful? Is his decision to put off his escape a capitulation or a victory? What does Niki discover in the dunes?

Acid the knowledge travellers draw. The world
Little and dull, today, tomorrow and
Tomorrow makes you see yourself—an appalled
Oasis in a tedium of sand.
Should we then go or stay? If you can, stay:
Go, if you must.[9]

—BAUDELAIRE

Niki's encounter with the sand is a learning process.
His first knowledge has been formal, scientific, lexical:

Sand: an aggregate of rock fragments. Sometimes
including loadstone, tinstone, and more rarely gold
dust. Diameter: 2 to 1/16 mm. (p. 13)

He soon notes other qualities: sand is fluid, almost life-
like, and destructive. "Like a living being it would creep
everywhere. The sands never rested. Gently but surely
they invaded and destroyed the surface of the earth" (p.
14). These thoughts in turn generate metaphysical questioning: why are people not fluid like the sand?

Certainly sand was not suitable for life. Yet, was a
stationary condition absolutely indispensable for
existence? Didn't unpleasant competition arise pre-
cisely because one tried to cling to a fixed condition?
If one were to give up a fixed position and abandon
oneself to the movement of the sands, competition
would soon stop. Actually, in the deserts flowers
bloomed and insects and other animals lived their
lives. These creatures were able to escape competition

[123]

through their great ability to adjust—for example, the man's beetle family.

While he mused on the effect of the flowing sands, he was seized from time to time by hallucinations in which he himself began to move with the flow. (p. 15)

One sees Baudelaire's "tedium of sand" also in the popular saying that an action is as useless as shoveling sand against the tide. Niki's version is similar: "Compared with a farmer's work, shoveling away the sand is like trying to pile up rocks in the River of Hades, where the devils cart them off as fast as you throw them in" (p. 188).[10] Niki's next encounter with the sand proves a jolt, for he realizes to his dismay that he must spend his days, or nights as it turns out, in just such an absurd activity. "The man was completely at a loss. He was bewildered, rather as if he had casually stepped on the tail of a snake that he had thought to be small but had turned out to be surprisingly large; by the time he had realized this, its head was already threatening him from behind." The existential significance too strikes him. "But this means you exist only for the purpose of clearing away the sand, doesn't it?" he asks the woman (p. 39). Her response reveals her adaptation to the communal purpose of the strange society. "The village keeps going because we never let up clearing away the sand like this. If we stopped, in ten days the village would be completely buried" (p. 39). Why then cling to the village? Perhaps because ultimately no one escapes the sand. Niki tries to sleep, but tosses restlessly, fatigued and feeling guilty because he left the woman to shovel by herself. "The same sand currents had swallowed up and destroyed flourishing cities and great empires," he muses; "the cities of antiquity, whose immobility no one doubted. . . . Yet, after all, they too were unable to resist the law of the flowing $\frac{1}{8}$-mm. sands. Sand. . . . sand was the antithesis of all form" (p. 41). His first efforts to overcome this flowing enemy end in failure; at the conclusion of part 1 Niki faints in the sand.

Niki's insight into the nature of sand continues to deepen. In part 2 he recalls a conversation he once had with the Möbius man when he had "sincerely tried revealing his inner thoughts." He objected to illusory education that makes one believe something is when it really isn't, he had told the Möbius man. He found sand particularly interesting, therefore, because "even though it's a solid, it has definite hydrodynamic properties." He had tried to elaborate. "The world is like sand," he said; the "fundamental nature of sand is very difficult to grasp when you think of it in its stationary state. Sand not only flows, but this very flow *is* the sand. . . . You yourself become sand. You see with the eyes of sand. Once you're dead you don't have to worry about dying any more" (p. 99). What he here expresses haltingly to the Möbius man he later picks up and expands upon when he sees a "ridge of dunes glistening and golden" and ponders the beauty of the sandscape at dusk. "What in heaven's name was the real essence of this beauty? Was it the precision of nature with its physical laws, or was it nature's mercilessness, ceaselessly resisting man's understanding?" He responds to his own questions that there was no reason to think of the life in the holes and the beauty of the landscape as being opposed to each other. Beautiful scenery need not be sympathetic to man. His own viewpoint in considering the sand to be a rejection of the stationary state was not madness . . . a $\frac{1}{8}$-mm. flow . . . a world where existence was a series of states. The beauty of sand, in other words, belonged to death. It was the beauty of death that ran through the magnificence of its ruins and its great power of destruction. (pp. 182–83)

One recalls the dictum of Wallace Stevens that "death is the mother of beauty" and, in connection with Niki's protest against "illusory education," Stevens's plea in "The Emperor of Ice Cream," "Let be be finale of seem." For "seeming" is the source of man's misery; it causes his "hell of loneliness." That loneliness, as Niki realizes, is "an unsatisfied thirst for illusion." Himself a victim, Niki recalls the endless repetition of breathing, walking, bowel movements, daily schedules, Sundays coming every seven days, and final exams after every four months which had driven him to nightmares in which he "was looking for a hiding place away from the eyes of people with a woman who had dirty fingernails." He had suddenly awakened to the "real," to "the heavens governed by an extremely simple elliptic cycle, and the sand dunes ruled by the $\frac{1}{8}$-mm. wavelengths" (p. 215).

What then is the sand? It is no less than existence, the fact of one's involvement with being, which presses relentlessly, insisting that one confront it. One can resist it, fighting compulsively, thirsting for an illusion of escape, or passively yield to it, bobbing like a cork, conceding its meaninglessness, or confront it, accept it, and forge from it a meaning. Especially, it is existence in time; for, above all, twentieth-century man is time-ridden. Time is the inescapable flux, the $\frac{1}{8}$-mm. flow, which is no respecter of persons. It invades every act, even the sexual encounter; it seeps into every corner of life, irritating, refusing to be ignored. It is the destroyer; it conquers cities. It is the enemy, for those who regard it so. But it is beautiful too, for those who see it so. And it is healing, soothing, even purifying (the woman cleans her plates in the sand). Abe's picture is complex; sand has many features. Its ambiguity is caught ironically in Niki's words when he tries to flee the village: "And yet, the sand compensated for sucking away one's strength by deadening the sound of footsteps" (p. 185). Time is ubiquitous, omnipresent, inescapable. To the heritage from the past (rosebuds in the West, cherry blossoms in the East) has been added that received from Henri Bergson, William James, and others to generate twentieth-century man's preoccupation with the ticking of the clock. Artists reflect the rebellious attempts to transcend it: Faulkner, scrambling the structure of *The Sound and the Fury*, blurring time by showing it through the mind of the idiot, Benjy; James Joyce, shaping his incredible *Finnegan's Wake* like a Viconian cycle, so the reader finishes the last sentence only to find himself at the beginning, piling multiple meanings and connotations on each word to break up the lineal-temporal tyranny of the printed line as if to spend time vertically, as Niki suggests to the

Möbius man (p. 180). Thus Abe's portrait of the red-eyed, sand-plagued Niki is a striking caricature of time-plagued modern man.

But Niki's journey into the self means confrontation not only with sand; there is also the sandwoman. He is involved not only with time, but the opposite sex. The latter, in fact, may be the primary factor (Abe titles his novel not *Sand,* but *The Woman of the Sand*). Perhaps Niki's nameless companion is a modern, earthy representative of the archetypal figures described long ago by Maud Bodkin.[11] Her patience and long-suffering, at any rate, clearly affect Niki, who worries whether or not he is obligated to her. What is difficult with regard to the novel's fantasy setting is in another way simple and elemental. Life is stripped of its numerous complications; a man and a woman confront each other and together confront the sand. Again Niki learns, and the learning brings change.

His education could hardly be called a course in sex education, yet the idea is not without merit, for the sex theme is prominent, and central to the book's meaning, not least of all in the contrast between Niki's experience with the sandwoman and the "other woman" he had known before. Niki's first shocked realization of his "imprisonment" is accompanied, ironically, by the arousal of sexual desire. Ironic too is the cause; it is ascribed to the action of the sand. "Yet, in spite of himself something not to be denied was welling up in his veins. The sand which clung to his skin was seeping into his veins and, from the inside, undermining his resistance" (p. 34). He regards his desire as a threat, and continues for some time to associate the thought of sexual intercourse with his bondage. The woman's crouching position sets him on edge. "When he left the woman's side he realized all the more how hazardous it was to be with her. No, he thought, the problem was not she herself, but that crouching position. He had never seen anything quite so indecent. It was out of the question to go back in to her. In every way that position of hers was exceedingly dangerous" (p. 54). Later, he even imagines her as part of some criminal conspiracy to trap him. "He couldn't relax his guard. Her charms were like some meat-eating plant, purposely equipped with the smell of sweet honey. First she would sow the seeds of scandal by bringing him to an act of passion, and then the chains of blackmail would bind him hand and foot" (p. 91).

His mistrust of the sandwoman harks back to his previous unsatisfactory experience with the "other woman," for there too he had felt trapped, defensive. With the other woman he had had, as he describes it to himself, "a somewhat obscure relationship in which, mutually at odds as they were, he could never be sure of her." In such a state, their passion had been lost, or rather, "they had frozen it by over-idealizing it" (p. 100). When the sandwoman queries, "City women are all pretty, aren't they?" Niki again recalls the other woman. "With his other woman, he had decided he would always use a condom. Even now he was not convinced that he had been completely cured of the venereal disease he had once had" (p. 132). The condom is indeed a "defense mechanism," and the woman rightly accuses him of having a "psychological venereal disease." Like time and death, venereal disease is no respecter of persons. It has left Niki spiritually as well as physically impotent. "And so his naked—hatless—member was paralyzed and useless" (p. 134). Sex has thus been for Niki a kind of "false promissory note," an experience full of suspicion and mistrust. He and his partner had so intellectualized and analyzed their actions that they had become detached observers, reflections of the real thing: "On that bed—with the other one—they had been a feeling man and woman, a watching man and woman; they had been a man who watched himself experiencing and a woman who watched herself experiencing; they had been a woman who watched a man watching himself and a man watching a woman watching herself . . . all reflected in counter-mirrors . . . the limitless consciousness of the sexual act" (pp. 140–41). With the sandwoman it is different. He "could not understand why he was so terribly attracted by her thighs. But he was . . . so much that he felt like taking the nerves of his body and coiling them one by one around them. The appetite of meat-eating animals must be just this—coarse, voracious. He fought back like a coiled spring. This was an experience he had not had with the other" (p. 140). Niki's encounter with the sandwoman is natural, instinctual.

Niki later violates this naturalness, first in a calculated seduction which he hopes, aided by sake and aspirin, will allow the woman to sleep and himself to escape. The falseness of his desire almost betrays him; the woman senses his deceit. "And so he reacted with even greater frenzy, spurring on his awakening senses. But there is a limit to perverted passion too. The woman who had been entreating him at first, manifested obvious fright at this frenzy" (p. 166). Niki almost fails in his effort. More flagrant is his last desperate effort to gain what he still imagines to be freedom. He strikes an obscene bargain with an old man of the village: a rope ladder in exchange for Niki's having sexual intercourse with the woman in the open where the old man and other workmen can watch. At this the heretofore passive woman revolts: "He heard a noise of cloth tearing, and at the same instant he was struck a terrible blow in the belly by the point of her shoulder, which bore the weight and anger of her whole body. He simply grasped his knees and bent in two. The woman, leaning over him, struck his face again and again with her fists" (p. 231). After the disappointed men have left, the beaten Niki abandons himself to the woman. He feels as if he has "turned into a liquid and melted into her body" (p. 232).

Niki is changed by his relationship with the woman. The original mistrust becomes concern, and when he is attempting to escape he wonders at length about the woman's actions, thoughts, and feelings; he wonders too if he has obligations: "She would smile bashfully as she groped for the lamp. But anyway, there was no reason for him to feel any obligation or responsibility for her smile. By his disappearance she would lose only a fragment of her life, one that could be easily replaced by a radio or a mirror." He knows better, however, for "what use would a mirror be to someone who no longer could be seen?" he asks rhetorically. After his desperate attempt to "bargain" for a rope ladder, Niki adjusts to the passing weeks and months and makes a discovery which injects excitement into the daily bout with the sand. The sand, he discovers, is an immense water pump. His crowtrap named "Hope," ignored by the crows, proves to be a suitable device for capturing moisture from the sand. When the woman is taken to the hospital with an extra-uterine pregnancy, and a rope ladder is left at the sand dwelling, Niki ponders briefly and decides to remain. His escape, he decides, can wait.

A number of recurring themes and ideas reinforce the meaning of Niki's confrontation with the woman and the dunes. One is the repeated reference to the trivia of every-day life, middle-class values, and actions which recur with meaningless monotony. Thus, after a week's absence Niki finds the newspaper "the same as usual." Its headlines are a study in frustration, crime, and violence: "Corporation Tax Bribery Spreads to City Officials. College Towns Become Industrial Meccas. . . . Mother Strangles Two Children: Takes Poison. Do Frequent Auto Thefts Mean New Mode of Life Breeds New Crime?" etc., etc. Reality, Niki thinks to himself, is a "gray canvas" with "miserable, unshaven fathers, shaking their complaining children by the shoulder trying to make them say it has been a pleasant Sunday . . . people's pathetic jealousy and impatience with others' happiness" (p. 98). The people in the dunes especially, he decides, are slaves, many of whom had lost all will to escape.

> He could easily understand how it was possible to live such a life. There were kitchens, there were stoves with fires burning in them, there were apple crates, in place of desks, piled full of books, there

were kitchens, there were sunken hearths, there were lamps, there were stoves with fires burning in them, there were torn shoji, there were sooty ceilings, there were kitchens, there were clocks that were running and clocks that weren't, there were blaring radios and broken radios, there were kitchens and stoves with fires in them. . . . It goes on, terrifyingly repetitive. One could not do without repetition in life, like the beating of the heart, but it was also true that the beating of the heart was not all there was to life. (pp. 176–77)

Niki must find just what else there is to life, for in the sand society he meets the tedium of everyday life in concentrated form. Significantly, it is from the sand itself that he gains the incentive which makes his ironically named project, "Hope," live up to its name.

Relatively uncomplicated as life in the dunes is, it nonetheless soon confronts Niki with the problem of obligation; the matter continually plagues his thoughts. His early hostility and defensiveness at the "outrage" of his imprisonment gives way to more sober reflection on the nature of involvement. He acknowledges the legitimacy of obligation in the human community, but can't see how it applies to his involuntary stay in the sand village. "Granted that obligation is a man's passport among his fellow men, why did he have to get a permit from the villagers? Human life shouldn't be so many bits of paper scattered about. . . . One can't get involved every time someone else is on the point of starvation. Damn it! He wanted water" (pp. 127–28). Niki might have continued the self-dialogue, as he so frequently does throughout the book. Thus he might have argued, "but starving people don't ask to starve; those born with a 'one-way' ticket don't ask to be born with a one-way ticket. Now you have a one-way ticket and are thirsty." In any case, Niki perceives the inevitable. If he is to have water, he must shovel sand.

The matter of obligation becomes more perplexing to Niki as time passes. His relationship with the sandwoman is particularly disturbing. There "had been no contract between him and her, and since there had been no contract there could be no breach of contract," he argues. But he remembers a multitude of little things—the cheap sake, the flesh on her thighs, her bashful smile—and concludes that "even if his involvement seemed unbelievable, it was nonetheless a fact" (pp. 190–91). Again, after trying repeatedly to discover why the woman remains in the sand dwelling, he decides "to leave off trying to figure out who was indebted to whom" (p. 193). Niki's scientific mind inclines him to the clearcut, precise definition, the black and white distinction. In the matter of obligation he is destined for frustration. When he and the woman discuss possible obligations between themselves, the village, and the outside, he ends "in a vague confusion and malaise." Nothing is clear: "His military map, on which enemy and friendly forces were supposed to be clearly defined, was blurred with unknowns of intermediate colors like indeterminate blobs of ink" (p. 224). The reader may be equally confused at this point. Perhaps Abe intends it this way; his goal may be to jar the reader from his usual track and make him rethink the entire structure of his relationships with others. At any rate, the end of the novel finds Niki with a "two-way" ticket, ostensibly free to leave. He chooses to remain, and presumably thereby acknowledges any obligations that decision may entail.

That final choice is in a significant way connected with water. The critic, conscious of countless literary spoofs about "water imagery," steps softly in such matters. But from the beginning of the narrative Niki has been especially intrigued by the "hydrodynamic" properties of sand. He puzzles over the mist; he argues with the woman concerning the rotting action of the sand. "Sand represents purity, cleanliness. Maybe it serves a preservative function, but there is certainly no question of its rotting anything," he declares dogmatically. A short time later the woman remarks that "everything really gets so damp because of the sand" (pp. 27–29). When he refuses to work, water is withheld. Frantic with thirst, he scrapes the wet sand from the bottom of the water jar and stuffs his mouth full, only to become nauseated and vomit. When the villagers finally deliver water, he acts like an animal. "When he came within reach of the bucket he pushed the woman aside, trampling her with his feet, and took hold of it with both hands. He could hardly take off the rope before he impatiently thrust his face into the bucket, his body heaving like a pump" (p. 148). That water should loom importantly in a story about sand is hardly strange, yet Abe's continued emphasis suggests a special significance, particularly in view of Niki's experiment, "Hope." What the crows reject, Niki accepts gleefully. His crow-trap turns out to be a relatively efficient water trap; he finds that the sand itself is "an immense pump." "He could scarcely contain his gradually rising excitement. There was only one answer he could think of. . . . It must be that the surface evaporation acted as a kind of pump, drawing up the subsurface water. When he thought about it, everything was easily explained—the enormous quantity of mist that came out of the dunes every morning and evening, the abnormal moisture which clung to the pillars and walls, rotting the wood" (p. 233). The discovery marks a change in Niki; he now passes the time with an inner excitement over his experiment. During this time the woman conceives. At the end of the novel, with the woman off to the hospital and Niki left alone, the protagonist's final action is to tend his experiment. "The water was piercingly cold. He sank down on his knees and remained inert, his hands still in the water" (p. 239 [Is it like prayer?]). Niki has already pondered the meaning. "The change in the sand corresponded to a change in himself," he muses. "Perhaps, along with the water in the sand, he had found a new self."

Perhaps he has. Perhaps he has found a new identity, free of the tyranny of time and illusion. He is no longer threatened by the tedium of everyday existence. Out of the apparent absurdity of life he has learned to extract meaning. He has been "set free" in the metaphysical sense, and "escape" is no longer necessary. The changes Niki undergoes suggest his new situation. When he first enters the sand community, he is acutely time-conscious. It is 8:02, he notes, then 11:16; the sound of the shovel and his own breathing "tick away the time." Then at 2:10 one day his watch stops. A newspaper for "Wednesday the 16th" confirms his awareness of the day, but he is no longer sure of the hour. Gradually, time ceases to dominate his thoughts. When he and the woman feel a mutual desire, he looks at her "with eyes in which time had ceased to run." "It's an accepted fact that time really goes horizontally," the Möbius man would have said, and if you try spending it vertically, you end up a mummy. Niki's attempt to escape is frustrated when he finds himself sinking in a sand bog, his body "fixed vertically in the sand." When he is rescued by the villagers, his "dreams, desperation, shame, concern with appearances" all remain "buried under the sand." Is Niki's frightening experience a symbolic death and rebirth signifying the end of time's tyranny? In any case, by the end of the novel what was at first ticked off minutely has blurred into months, seasons (November, March, spring), and, according to the final legal notice, years. Niki is no longer time-ridden.

Nor is his vision the same. An entomologist, Niki has come in search of insect specimens. Should he find a new type, he would achieve a measure of ephemeral fame. His name, Abe comments wryly, would be "perpetuated in the memory of his fellow men by being associated with an insect" (p. 10). The almost laughable nature of such "fame" is suggested by the technical name of a double-winged garden beetle, the *Cicindela japonica Motschulsky*. Not so laughable is the fact that Niki's way of observing insects had become his way of observing people (ironically, at one point Niki likens his own situation in the sand to being snared "exactly like a mouse or an insect" p. 51). He had analyzed his colleagues and the "other woman" as if they were specimens. Like Hawthorne's Chillingworth, he had been cold, detached, scientifically "heartless."[12] "To eyes with magnifying lenses everything seemed tiny and insectlike. The little ones crawling around over there were his colleagues having a cup of tea in the faculty room. The one in this corner was the other woman, naked, on a dampish bed, her eyes half closed, motionless although the ash of her cigarette was about to fall." He regarded them as cookie molds which have "only edges and no insides." But Niki has changed. "If the chance occurred for him to renew his relationship with them" he realizes, "he would have to start all over again from the very beginning" (p. 236).

Thus Jumpei Niki becomes free, a kind of existential hero carrying his twin burdens of despair and freedom, but no longer crushed under them like the horse in the cartoon, broken under the big bruiser, which had sent him into hysterics. Once time-ridden, he is time-free; once cold and analytical, he now anguishes over the woman's feelings; once a victim of "psychological VD," he now enjoys the woman "hatless," and they conceive a child. Niki has made the hard journey into the depths of his consciousness and emerged a "person." The official notice is thus an ironic and humorous twist: what is missing to the time-ridden "outside" world—seven years is "official death"—is found. Perhaps, then, Abe's use of humor and irony deserve the final word. The satiric touches, humorous anecdotes, and ironies—including the final legal notice—suggest that the discovery of one's identity should be accompanied by a sense of humor. If twentieth-century man is time-ridden, he is also introspective, prone to take himself too seriously. One should acknowledge with good grace that this applies to critics as well. Abe's simple, abrupt, almost disconnected style came upon the Japanese literary scene with considerable freshness. To have engaged a reader with this style, to have drawn him into a narrative, and to have engrossed him in the hero's adventures is a considerable accomplishment. To again indulge the Western penchant for finding a "meaning" may be to act like a literary entomologist, treating the work of art like an insect. To be able to chuckle at oneself is to approach real personhood; such happy discoveries, like Niki's, are not recorded in official statistics.

8

A NEW HERO

There is an archetypal appeal about Bird, the diminutive
hero of Kenzaburo Oe's *A Personal Matter*.[1] It is that of
the underdog, the little hero, the embattled champion
confronting the overwhelming size of the giant enemy
yet enduring and prevailing to victory. It is an appeal
which transcends national boundaries and which the
folktales, legends, and even comic strips of countless
peoples illustrate. From the Biblical David, slaying the
huge Goliath, to the contemporary American cartoon
hero Mighty Mouse, to the Japanese children's tale of
Little One Inch, one sees—and partakes in—the over-
coming of odds, the miraculous or near-miraculous
triumph of small and few over large and many. The
psychological appeal is deep; it roots in man's hope that
despite appearances, or even current conditions, right will
prevail over might, light over darkness. It is an affirmation, an insistence, that order will prevail over chaos.

But though the image of the small hero is almost universally admired, it has special appeal for the Japanese, whose history records their consciousness, especially in modern times, of being a small island nation surrounded by much larger rivals who all too frequently proved threatening. Thus in the Russo-Japanese and Sino-Japanese wars, artists and chroniclers heralded the triumph of the outnumbered but heroic servants of the emperor who overcame the enemy, sometimes hurling themselves like "human bullets."[2] Never was the idea more relevant than at present when the Japanese find themselves sandwiched between the postwar "giants," Soviet Russia, Communist China, and the United States, and yet challenging them, at least in the economic arena.[3] One remembers too that the Japanese are smaller in stature than the average Western counterpart, and that for two and a half decades since the end of the war in the Pacific they have suffered the taller forms of American soldiers, businessmen, and other representatives of the occupier conspicuously showing on the commuter trains. The triumph of the small hero is indeed an appealing notion. The ancient art of jujutsu, or its modern form of judo, is, among other things, a way by which a small person can overcome a large person, or even two or three. A Japanese friend recalls vividly the picture he saw some years ago in a children's book, of a diminutive Japanese judo expert engaged in a match with a huge Russian wrestler before the Czar of Russia. The Russian opponent had been flipped into midair by his smaller but more skillful antagonist.

But Japan also shares with its huge neighbors in another experience of bigness, for this Jack-the-Giant-Killer in the world of commerce has accomplished an astounding feat in the postwar years akin to the similar "economic miracle" of West Germany. The Japanese "salary man" now must face the anxieties created by involvement in huge corporate structures, the threat of becoming a soulless cog in the complex, fast-moving machinery of a technological society. Contemporary cartoons celebrate the dilemma of such "little" men, showing the tiny figure labeled "taxpayer" surrounded by frightening giants which demand his pay; or again, the small, bewildered office worker stares in dismay at the huge, leering faces and grasping mechanical arms of computers. Amid the stresses of such a society and such bigness, a man may well lose his bearings, or, as Kobo Abe testifies in both *The Woman in the Dunes* and *The Ruined Map,* the outlines of one's identity may become an unreadable confusion.[4] Takahashi-san (which may serve as an equivalent of John Doe) must now confront the giant.

Small wonder that Oe's hero is popular. Nor is it strange that the novel once again records a quest for identity, for Bird must, in a complex, threatening world, find himself, convince himself of his role as a man, locate himself on the human map. The novel's central theme is this search for an acceptable self-image; Bird, from the opening pages, is concerned with his identity. "No choice but living with the same face and posture from fifteen to sixty-five, was he that kind of person?" he asks at the beginning of the novel (p. 4). His brief series of adventures records the answer: a change, an initiation into manhood, a growing out of self-preoccupation into mature responsi-

bility. Birds are fashioned for flight; at the end of the novel
the hero has outgrown his childish nickname.

What sort of a hero, then, is Bird?

> Bird paused to gaze at himself in the wide, darkly
> shadowed display window. . . . Bird, twenty-seven
> years and four months old. He had been nicknamed
> "Bird" when he was fifteen, and he had been Bird
> ever since: the figure awkwardly afloat like a
> drowned corpse in the inky lake of window glass
> still resembled a bird. He was small and thin. . . . He
> slouched forward when he walked and bunched his
> shoulders around his neck; his posture was the same
> when he was standing still. . . . His tan, sleek nose
> thrust out of his face like a beak and hooked sharply
> toward the ground. His eyes gleamed with a hard,
> dull light the color of glue. . . . His thin, hard lips
> were always stretched tightly across his teeth; the
> lines from his high cheekbones to his chin described
> a sharply pointed V. And hair licking at the sky like
> ruddy tongues of flame. (pp. 3–4)

The physical description marks Bird as distinctively
modern, the hero replete with such antiheroic qualities
as physical flaws and (as it turns out) psychological tics, as
well as a penchant for introspection. One can sympathize
and identify with such a fellow traveler in his weakness.
But Bird's compensating qualities are even more appealing. In his younger days, Bird has been a feared brawler.
The fighting spirit of the samurai is apparent; *bushido,*

the way of the warrior, is assimilated under modern dress.[5] Bird is of course knowing, wise in the shadowy, tough ways of the world. He is unabashed, consequently, by a transvestite or a fag bar; he is frightened but cleverly calculating when cornered by a gang of tough teen-age hoodlums. And he possesses sensitivity, that trait which makes a near-artist of so many modern heroes (and readers). Bird's distress when he attempts to make love with Himiko illustrates. It is not a sign of his inability, for he proves able after all; his problem marks, rather, his sensitive search for self-understanding. Indeed his success in satisfying Himiko suggests a crucial change in Bird, from the self-preoccupied and hence near-impotent to the less selfish and hence competent. The sensitivity is reinforced in other ways too. Bird feels some guilt for having abandoned the young Kikuhiko, who subsequently becomes a homosexual. His feeling shows not only his sensitivity to others, but helps counterbalance the emphasis on Bird as victim of an irrational fate in the form of his abnormal baby. Even his desire to flee to Africa, though it is in part an escape wish, is a sign of sensitivity, the mark of the dreamer, of one who refuses to accept dully whatever circumstances bring. And Bird is intelligent; a teacher capable in the academic world, he yet resists its pretenses (he has quit graduate school). He is an angry young man, incensed at the pointlessness of the trap he finds himself in, an honest rebel who refuses to call the mess he vomits on the schoolroom floor anything but what it is, the aftermath of a massive hangover. Yet Bird proves himself ultimately responsible; pragmatically fortifying himself with something called "forbear-

ance," he transfers his sensitive fighting spirit to a larger
battleground than his own inner world.

The transfer suggests the irony of Oe's title, *A Personal
Matter*. The Japanese original, *Kojinteki na Taiken,* has the
meaning of personal and private, with perhaps secondary
overtones of uniqueness and depth. It is of course very
much a "personal" affair, a matter of Bird's identity as a
person. It is unique not only in the sense that every
personal experience is by definition unique, but in the
dramatic, almost bizarre nature of the experience. In
another sense, however, it is not merely personal but
inter-personal. A bird, however much one may admire
its qualities, is not a human. Oe's hero too must learn to
become a person, which is to say that he must learn to
identify himself with other persons. His obsession with
himself and the seeming injustice of his fate must give
way to a more human concern or it will end in isolation
and flight. But his initiatory steps take him first deep
within himself and then out of himself into an inter-
personal world where not only one's self, but one's relationship to other selves is supremely important. Thus
Bird's affair is not only "personal" and private, but involves his personhood, and more, the very nature of
society as a group of interrelated persons. Bird recalls his
four-week drunk the summer following his marriage.
"He was like a mental incompetent with only the slightest chance of recovery, but he had to tame all over again
not only the wilderness inside himself, but the wilderness
of his relations to the world outside" (p. 7). Thus, in its
modernity as well as its hints of archetype, Oe's narrative
is very much a universal matter.

The birth of Bird's first child, an abnormal baby, precipitates his rebellious quest. For Bird, the strange object he glimpses in the hospital proves an ontological shock and he feels emasculated, stripped of his manhood. The baby with its suspected brain hernia is an appropriate symbol for an intellectually warped society; it suggests the unnatural product of an unnatural environment. There is too much head; the unstated implication, which applies to Bird, is that there may not be enough heart. Bird's reaction, expressed primarily in sexual terms, is equally appropriate. In his room, he gazes at his shriveled sex organ in dismay. Later, Himiko accuses him with the truth. "And the women you slept with probably felt self-pity and disgust, too. I bet it was never completely satisfying, was it, Bird?" (p. 115). His problem is how to recover his manhood or, in terms of the title, his role as a person. Bird and the baby at the beginning of the novel are both warped; at the end, they are becoming natural. The suspected hernia turns out to be a benign tumor; Bird's self-preoccupation becomes a responsible concern for others. Thus Bird and the baby are closely identified, a fact underscored throughout the novel by Bird's imitations of the child. In Himiko's bed he curls up "naked as a baby, defenseless," and after seeing his infant attempt to scratch above his ears, Bird compulsively duplicates the action. Oe maintains a careful balance or planned ambiguity with regard to the baby's role in relation to Bird. For an abnormal child is on the one hand an irrational event, a bolt of fate beyond one's control. On the other hand it is a part of its father, and the deep shame Bird suffers, and which the reader is first tempted to regard as unwarranted, proves to be only too appropriate after all. Thus Bird is in part victim of circumstances beyond his control, but only in part; he is also self-victimized, as his close identification with the baby hints. Oe suggests that ultimately much of the responsibility is Bird's; to fail to accept it would be to deny himself. To destroy the child would be to commit spiritual suicide.

In his opening chapter Oe introduces major themes and hints at the novel's outcome. The narrative opens with Bird gazing at a map of Africa in a showcase.

> The continent itself resembled the skull of a man who had hung his head. With doleful, downcast eyes, a man with a huge head was gazing at Australia. . . . The miniature Africa indicating population distribution in a lower corner of the map was like a dead head beginning to decompose; another, veined with transportation routes, was a skinned head with the capillaries painfully exposed. Both these little Africas suggested unnatural death, raw and violent. (pp. 1–2)

Africa has a complex symbolic function for Bird. It represents, of course, a wish-fantasy, a place of escape, and the maps Bird purchases and pins to the wall above the bed signify what he regards as a ticket to freedom. But Oe's metaphors suggest a deeper significance. The showcase map hints at both Bird and the baby: the latter in the reiterated head-shape (skull, huge head, dead head, skinned head), Bird in the reference to the "man who had hung his head," and both in the reference to "unnatural death." Bird's first look at his baby reveals the "large and abnormal" head, and throughout the novel Bird suffers from shame. One suspects, then, that Africa is as much Bird's own dark inner world as it is the Dark Continent, as much the unnatural society he is trapped in as the rapidly changing land of his dreams, and that his desire to go there is at its deepest level as much his desire to triumph over his own circumstances as an escape through flight. The suspicion is confirmed by a nightmare Bird has in which what he has called the "fear that roots in the backlands of the unconscious" (p. 6) takes shape. Curled up in bed "like a threatened sow bug, or, one can add, like a foetus, Bird dreams of being chased by a giant warthog across a plain in West Africa. "I've come to Africa unequipped and with no training; I cannot escape," he thinks in his dream. He awakens to the ringing of the phone just as the animal's teeth close sharply on his ankle (p. 20). Bird, like so many of his contemporary peers, feels trapped. Like John Updike's Rabbit, his impulse is to run. Unlike that protagonist, however, Bird finally decides to remain. But the nightmare portrays his deepest fears; the African terrain is a mixture of his own troubled psyche and a malignant society. In the dream, the blue line which he thinks is a place of safety turns out to be only a game refuge which would not have deterred the warthog in the least. In other words, there is no escape. There is nothing to do but stand and fight.

That this is what Bird will do is foreshadowed in the opening chapter where he encounters the gang of teen-age toughs. Through a combination of quick wit, courage, and his own toughness, Bird manages to escape with only minor bruises. The episode is a microcosm of the novel's overall plot; Bird is shamed, suffers, but, with his back to the wall, faces his problem head-on and wins a victory. For Bird is a fighter, at war within and without. The hostility he envisions on every hand is matched by his inner doubts. He projects the antagonism in his dream, he faces it unexpectedly in the persons of the young hoodlums, and he senses it in his surroundings, as when he bicycles to the hospital: "The feeling of futile flight in his dream returned. But he raced on. His shoulder snapped a slender ginkgo branch and the splintered end sprang back and cut his ear. Even so, Bird didn't slow up. Raindrops that whined like bullets grazed his throbbing ear" (p. 22). The doctors appear hostile too. There is "something suspicious" about the director, and "this hairy, middle-aged doctor prevented him from letting down his guard. As if, deep beneath that hirsute skin, something potentially lethal was trying to rear its bushy head and was being forcibly restrained" (p. 23). But the hospital, especially, emphasizes Bird's minuscule stature and vulnerability. He feels like David in Goliath land. "Bird started across the hospital square, wide and long as a soccer field. Halfway, he turned around and looked up at the building where he had just abandoned his first child, a baby on the brink of death. A gigantic building, with an overbearing presence, like a fort. Glistening in the sunlight of early summer, it made the baby who was faintly screaming in one of its obscure corners seem meaner than a grain of sand" (p. 39). Bird's sensitive spirit records animosity throughout his trials. Repeatedly, he refers to his own child as Apollinaire, "wounded on a . . . battlefield," his head in bandages (p. 33).[6] All the babies in the intensive care unit of the hospital seem like "wee, feeble prisoners" (p. 92). In his anger and frustration, Bird longs to repay hostility in kind. He envisions the "ultimate in anti-social sex," and at one point has a drunken desire to "butcher and rape the corpse" (pp. 65, 104). At times his frustration makes him regard even his helpless infant as an enemy—a "deadly cactus," or a "monster"—and he braces himself for "battle" (pp. 95, 99). All of this hostility suggests that for Bird fight is a metaphor of life, and that he must struggle against great odds, combating the irrational forces which threaten him within and without. His very identity is at stake. Though his first impulse is to run, Bird fights. "If I don't fight now," he reasons when trapped by the gang, "I'll not only lose the chance to go to Africa forever, my baby will be born into the world solely to lead the worst possible life" (p. 16). Since Africa and the baby are parts of Bird, representing the complexity of his relationship to his own inner self and society, Bird's decision has an ironic significance beyond his awareness. It adumbrates his later choice. This contemporary antiheroic samurai will prevail after all.

His triumph has a primitive, earthy appeal. It is a gory moment, but there is a healthy naturalness to Bird's action when he reawakens to the "joy of battle" and drives "like a ferocious bull" into his attacker's belly (p. 16). The action contrasts with the unhealthy, unnaturalness of the "outlandish establishment" where Bird first encounters the gang. Appropriately named "Gun Corner," this strange place suggests the hostility as well as the grotesque unnaturalness of society. Indeed it is a miniature world, with "paper flags of the United Nations." On a giant sign, a cowboy crouches with pistol flaming, his spurs pinning down the head of an Indian. Inside, bizarre machines glare at the patrons. There is a miniature forest on a conveyor belt, a machine where an E-type Jaguar speeds forever down a suburban highway on a painted belt of scenery, and an Iron Maiden, "twentieth-century model": "A beautiful, life-sized maiden of steel with mechanical red-and-black stripes was protecting her bare chest with stoutly crossed arms. The player attempted to pull her arms away from her chest for a glimpse of her hidden metal breasts; his grip and pull appeared as numbers in the windows which were the maiden's eyes" (p. 11).

Bird's trouble with the mechanical maiden—he scores only the average grip and pull of a forty-year-old—indicates that he has been unmanned. This is underscored by his reaction to the baby's birth. Thus his quest for identity is to a large degree expressed in terms of sexuality. Much of the quest takes place in the apartment of Himiko, an old girl friend from university days. Bird's sojourn with Himiko serves a number of functions, and the apartment, like the Golden Temple in Mishima's novel, becomes the symbol of a complex psychological experience. In the first place, the messy apartment—Bird has to step in, over, or around the debris in order to cross the room —is an emblem of chaos, reflecting the confusion, frustration, and rebellion in the minds of both Bird and Himiko. For Bird, the confusion shows in his deep-rooted fears over his sexual role. Shamed by the birth of his abnormal child and the symbolic experience in the "Gun Corner" (the name suggests yet another sexual indicator), Bird needs to assert his masculinity, but finds his desire matched by his dread. Bird seems to suffer from a kind of castration complex, and is at first unable to satisfy Himiko or achieve orgasm himself except in a perverse way. "I'm afraid of the dark recesses where that grotesque baby was created," he admits (p. 107), but there is more. Bird's father has committed suicide, one learns, and the fact that Himiko's frustration is due to her young husband's also having killed himself suggests the complexity of Oe's delineation here. Himiko, with keen insight, charges Bird with never having had satisfactory sexual relations.

Bird thus needs both to satisfy and be satisfied by Himiko. In part his desire is an escape, a retreat to the womb, for the "dark recesses" are a place of comfort as well as fear. The idea is supported by Himiko's quasi-maternal role, chiding, advising, comforting (as well as her physical appearance). "At a time like this you must be careful to have someone comfort you almost more than you need at least once," she says soothingly at one point (p. 114). But Oe's metaphors suggest that the womb is more a symbolic place of self-discovery than of escape or comfort. And Bird's tendency to identify with his baby adds to the notion. "You curled up like an infant and clenched your fists and started bawling in your sleep. Waagh! Waagh! Your face was all mouth," Himiko informs him after he dreams (p. 155). Again his desire is matched by fear of what he might encounter. "I have this feeling there's what you'd call another universe back in there," he says. "It's dark, it's infinite, it's teeming with everything anti-human: a grotesque universe. . . . my fear has certain resemblances to an astronaut's fantastic acrophobia!" (p. 110). The discovery motif becomes more explicit later when Bird likens his experience to being in a cave like Tom Sawyer, but without Tom's success. "He had to suffer in a pitch-black cave, but at the same time he found his way out into the light he also found a bag of gold! . . . my Tom Sawyer is at the bottom of a desperately deep mine shaft and I wouldn't be surprised if he went mad!" Bird exclaims in a moment of depression (p. 155).

But his initiation into self-discovery and maturity is more hopeful than he imagines at the time. One of the signs is his display of honesty in refusing to acknowledge his fit of vomiting in front of the cram school class to be other than it is (the vomit is likened to an African panorama!); another is his later success in sexually satisfying Himiko, when, for once, he acts selflessly in accord with another's needs. His sexual coming-of-age is an important step toward maturity. Another is his encounter with Delchef, the foreign legation member who has secluded himself in the back alleys of Tokyo's Shinjuku district with a "young delinquent." Delchef is "not disillusioned politically with his own country, not planning spy activity or hoping to defect." He is "simply unable to take leave of this particular Japanese girl" (p. 140). Delchef's action is unconventional, but deeply human in terms of personal involvement. He defies international protocol, but affirms a human tie. Bird's mission—he has agreed to reason with Delchef—suggests again a trip to the visceral depths for self-discovery. In a cul-de-sac "shaped like a stomach" Bird finds his friend and receives his last lesson in personhood. Delchef inquires about

Bird's baby, Bird tries to explain, and Delchef rebukes him. "Are you rejecting your baby?" he asks. This time the attack comes from a friend. "Bird felt as if he had been downed by a bullet of criticism from an unexpected sniper. He gathered himself to protest at whatever the cost and suddenly hung his head, sensing he had nothing to say to Mr. Delchef. 'Ah, the poor little thing!' Mr. Delchef said in a whisper. Bird looked up, shuddering, and realized the foreigner was talking not about his baby but about him" (p. 166).

Bird's quest is of course not yet ended. During his stay with Himiko he has run the gamut of anxiety, experiencing by turns self-pity, shame, hostility, and masochistic urges; Bird's wife challenges his self-centeredness when she wonders if he is "the type of person who abandons someone weak" when that person needs him most (p. 129). The surface reference is to Kikuhiko, the young man who had become homosexual. And the wife's suspicions almost prove true, as Bird in a last desperate regression plans with Himiko to have a quack doctor kill the baby and then to flee to Africa, thus abandoning wife, child, and responsibility. Significantly, Bird and Himiko attempt to complete their plan in Himiko's red MG, apt image of her rebellious frustration. Like the "pluralistic universe" with which she tries to rationalize her despair, the red sports-car is a pathetic form of escape. It can also be death-dealing, and the mission on which Bird and Himiko use it involves not only the infant but their own spiritual being. With its black hood on top of its scarlet body, the car appears "like the torn flesh of a wound and the scabs around it" (p. 185). But with radio news reports of Soviet nuclear testing providing an ironic international background music to his own destructive urges, Bird decides to leave Himiko and his dreams of Africa, and claims his child.

Some critics find the end of the novel disappointing. "He takes responsibility and, in a weak ending, that is that," says Edward Seidensticker, adding that the conclusion is "comfortingly positive—and not really very convincing."[7] Part of the trouble may lie in the abruptness of Bird's about-face. Oe tries, at least, to prepare the reader for the outcome by hints in the form of Bird's initiatory steps and by symbolic foreshadowings such as the fight with the teen-age gang. More important, however, is what the outcome suggests. The novel has been interpreted as an allegory of Japan's growth to maturity among nations, as well as a dramatization of the "essentially solitary and withdrawn nature" of one's existential choice.[8] There is something Japanese in the feisty hero's sublimated samurai spirit, but there is more that transcends national interests. Bird, like a number of modern heroes, plumbs the depths of the existential pit only to emerge aware that one's existence involves other existences, that self-suffering is ultimately self-destructive. The family to which Bird returns at the end, one suspects, is not so much Japanese as simply human, the matter not so much private as personal in a universal way. Contemporary man, dwarfed and threatened by the grotesque complexity of life, and bolstered more with forbearance than bravado, can yet be a man. At the end of the novel Bird resolves to reverse his old fantasy and "be the native guide, for the foreigners who come to Japan" (p. 214).

Any tour he offers will doubtless include monuments indicating that Japan's literary art, in its ability to combine something of the Japanese spirit, the modern quest for identity, and the universal need for human involvement, is a rising sun.

NOTES

CHAPTER ONE

1. See Munesuke Mita, "Patterns of Alienation in Contemporary Japan," *Journal of Social and Political Ideas in Japan* (renamed *The Japan Interpreter*), vol. 5, nos. 2–3, December 1967, pp. 139–78. Primary translator Robert Epp provides valuable information in his notes, pp. 172–77. See also Hidetoshi Kato, "A Content Analysis of Life Counseling Columns," *Japanese Popular Culture*, comp. and trans. Hidetoshi Kato, Tuttle, Tokyo, 1959, pp. 60–75.

2. Mita, "Patterns of Alienation," p. 140.

3. Ibid., pp. 152–53.

4. Ibid., pp. 154–55.

5. Ibid., pp. 158–59.

6. For a contemporary Japanese example, the Emerald Cloud Breeze Tribe, see *Transpacific*, no. 3, 1970, p. 55.

7. Mita, "Patterns of Alienation," p. 171.

8. Katherine Hondius, ed., *Identity: Stories for This Generation*, Scott, Foresman, Chicago, 1966, p. viii.

9. Haruo Umezaki, "Sakurajima," trans. D. E. Mills, *The*

Shadow of Sunrise: Selected Stories of Japan and the War, comp. Shoichi Saeki, Kodansha International, Tokyo, 1966, p. 102.

10. An attempt to explain to themselves, and perhaps to the world, the remarkable development of their economy is illustrated by a recent two-volume study, *Nihonjin no Keizai Kodo* (Economic Behavior of the Japanese), ed. Mikio Sumiya, Oriental Economist, Tokyo, 1969. It draws on materials presented by scholars, economists, jurists, businessmen, and industrialists in a series of culture symposiums.

11. Mita, "Patterns of Alienation," p. 166.

12. *Japan Times,* Sunday, March 8, 1970.

13. Ibid., Friday, February 20, 1970.

14. Ichiro Kawasaki, *Japan Unmasked,* Tuttle, Tokyo, 1969, pp. 18, 228.

15. See the policy speeches of Prime Minister Eisaku Sato and Foreign Minister Kiichi Aichi before the sixty-third session of the Diet, Saturday, February 14, 1970. Carried in translation in the *Japan Times,* Sunday, February 15, 1970.

16. See, for example, the remarks of Edwin O. Reischauer in the *Japan Times,* Monday, March 2, 1970.

17. *Journal of Social and Political Ideas in Japan* (renamed *The Japan Interpreter*) vol. 5, nos. 2–3, December 1967, is devoted to "university and society" and contains extensive criticisms of the present system.

18. This particular example comes from Tokyo Women's Christian College. A study of student graffiti might prove illuminating.

19. See *Japan Times,* Wednesday, February 11, 1970.

20. *Sazae-san* is carried in newspapers and is also available in collected form.

21. *Sato Sampei Shu* (Cartoons of Sato Sampei), Chikuma Shobo, Tokyo, 1969.

22. Though dated, Miss Benedict's classic study (*The Chrysanthemum and the Sword,* Houghton Mifflin, New York, 1946) is still valuable.

23. John K. Fairbank, Edwin O. Reischauer, and Albert M. Craig, *East Asia: The Modern Transformation,* Houghton Mifflin, Boston, 1965, p. 830. This book contains extensive bibliographical suggestions.

24. Ibid., pp. 828–29.

25. See, for example, *The Japanese Image,* ed. Maurice Schneps and Alvin D. Coox, Orient/West, Tokyo, 1965. Earl Miner, Edward Seidensticker, and Ivan Morris contributed articles concerning translation problems.

26. Ibid., pp. 290–98.

27. Edward Seidensticker, "The Unshapen Ones," *Japan Quarterly,* vol. 2, 1964, pp. 64–69.

28. Jun Eto, "An Undercurrent in Modern Japanese Literature," *Journal of Asian Studies,* vol. 23, no. 3, May 1964, p. 435. See also Howard Hibbett, "The Portrait of the Artist in Japanese Fiction," *Far Eastern Quarterly,* vol. 14, no. 3, May 1955, pp. 347–54.

29. Roethke's poem is included in a popular anthology published in Japan, *American Poetry: An Anthology,* ed. Rikutaro Fukuda and Motoshi Karita, Kinseido, Tokyo, 1965.

30. Margaret Mead, *Male and Female: A Study of the Sexes in a Changing World.* First published in U.S.A., 1950. I quote from the Pelican edition, Penguin Books, Harmondsworth, Middlesex, England, 1962, p. 180.

CHAPTER TWO

1. Fumiko Hayashi, "Bones," trans. Ted Takaya, *The Shadow of Sunrise: Selected Stories of Japan and the War,* comp. Shoichi Saeki, Kodansha International, Tokyo, 1966, p. 143.

2. See Montaigne's "On the Cannibals" and Norman Mailer's *Cannibals and Christians*.

3. Cf. Leslie A. Fiedler, *The Return of the Vanishing American*, Stein & Day, New York, 1968, pp. 29–49.

4. Newspapers carried accounts of cannibalism among the starving victims of the Biafra-Nigeria conflict. See, for example, "Biafra's Last Days Saw Cannibalism," *The Japan Times*, Feb. 4, 1970, p. 4. In American history cannibalism occurred among members of the Donner party (1846–47), a group of immigrants to California that, trapped by an early snow, suffered greatly from cold and lack of food.

5. Tadashi Moriya, *No Requiem,* trans. Geoffrey S. Kishimoto, Hokuseido, Tokyo, 1968; Shohei Ooka, *Fires on the Plain,* trans. Ivan Morris, Knopf, New York, 1967; Taijun Takeda, *Luminous Moss,* in *This Outcast Generation and Luminous Moss,* trans. Yusaburo Shibuya and Sanford Goldstein, Tuttle, Tokyo, 1967. References to these works are included by page number in the text.

6. Lu Shun, "The Dairy of a Madman," *Ah Q and Others: Selected Stories of Lu Shun,* trans. Wang Chi-shen, Columbia U. Pr., 1941. Another taboo, incest, may be suggested here under the guise of a "principle of filial piety."

7. In the interest of simplicity, I have left uncorrected occasional oddities in the quotations from *No Requiem. Karabaw* should be *carabao.*

8. Any two or all three of these books would provide a stimulating comparative study for teaching purposes. See also Ashihei Hino, *Barley and Soldiers,* trans. K. and L. W. Bush, 2d ed., Kenkyusha, Tokyo, 1939. This popular diary-novel of a soldier in the China campaign, written during a time of victorious conquest, shows another attitude.

9. Cf. William Golding's *Lord of the Flies.*

10. The works of Mircea Eliade offer fascinating commen-

tary on "ritual cannibalism." In *Myths, Dreams, and Mysteries* (Harper & Row, New York, 1960, pp. 197–200), he summarizes the "characteristic features of initiation." The fifth (last) feature is the "injunction to kill." Head-hunting and cannibalism are parts of this scheme. To kill and eat a man is to imitate behavior of the gods and hence is a "religious act." War itself is "a decadent ritual in which a holocaust of innumerable victims is offered up to the gods of victory."

11. Cf. Ooka's hero, Private Tamura, whose identity problems suggest the same polar possibilities.

12. Takeda fails to understand Ooka in this connection and overlooks the significance of point of view. He accuses Ooka of "smug complacency" because "the hero of *Fires on the Plain* assures himself he is civilized by reflecting that 'I did kill, but I didn't eat' " (*Luminous Moss*, pp. 113–14). Tamura does, in fact, eat human flesh, and knows it, though it is not the flesh of someone he himself has killed. More significantly, Tamura is distraught from hunger and disease, and suffers hallucinations and confusion of identity. Takeda's superficial judgment misses the irony in Tamura's statements.

CHAPTER THREE

1. Masuji Ibuse, *Black Rain*, trans. John Bester, Kodansha International, Tokyo, 1969. All references are included in the text by page number.

2. *Hiroshima* originally appeared in *The New Yorker* (1946). I quote from the convenient Bantam edition (New York, 1948). All references are included in the text by page number.

3. A good beginning bibliography and other material are available in Robert Jungk's *Children of the Ashes: The Story of a Rebirth*, trans. Constantine Fitzgibbon, Harcourt, Brace and World, New York, 1961. See also Robert Lifton's *Death in Life: Survivors of Hiroshima* (Random House, New York,

1969) for bibliography and treatment of psychic reactions of Hiroshima survivors.

4. The time lines blur again in regard to Yasuko; her "present" illness is a delayed radiation sickness.

5. The meticulous attention to details concerning the dead Mrs. Taka Mitsuda represents another kind of affirmation. The victim's height, chromium-plated false teeth, personal possessions, and even known details of her husband's career are carefully noted. See pp. 140–41.

6. See, for example, *We Japanese,* selected by Fujiya Hotel, Ltd., Yamagata Press, Yokohama, n.d., p. 58.

7. See *In Our Time.* Trout fishing also figures importantly in *The Sun Also Rises.*

8. See Ruth Benedict's *Chrysanthemum and the Sword,* Houghton Mifflin, New York, 1946.

CHAPTER FOUR

1. Jiro Osaragi, *Homecoming,* trans. Brewster Horwitz, Knopf, New York, 1954. All references are included in the text by page number.

2. Edwin O. Reischauer, comment on the jacket.

3. See Taiko Hirabayashi, "Modern Japanese Literature," *The Oriental Economist,* July 1962, p. 419.

4. Snell Putney and Gail J. Putney, *The Adjusted American: Normal Neuroses in the Individual and Society,* Harper Colophon Books, New York, 1966, p. 176.

5. See pp. 41, 254, 287, 295.

6. Conversation with the author, Tokyo, February 3, 1969.

7. See Eric Berne, *Games People Play,* Grove Press, New York, 1964.

CHAPTER FIVE

1. Yukio Mishima, *The Temple of the Golden Pavilion,* trans.

Ivan Morris, Knopf, New York, 1959. All references are included in the text by page number.

2. Cited by Nancy Wilson Ross in the introduction to *The Temple of the Golden Pavilion,* p. vii.

3. A movie, *Enjo,* was made from the novel.

4. Yukio Mishima, *Forbidden Colors,* trans. Alfred H. Marks, Knopf, New York, 1968; idem, *Confessions of a Mask,* trans. Meredith Weatherby, New Directions, New York, 1958; idem, *The Sailor Who Fell from Grace with the Sea,* trans. John Nathan, Knopf, New York, 1965.

5. See Louise Duus, "The Novel as Koan: Mishima Yukio's *The Temple of the Golden Pavilion,*" *Critique,* vol. 10, no. 2, pp. 120–29. The *koan* idea is intriguing, but nowhere does Miss Duus state a clear thesis.

6. See, for example, George W. Kisker, *The Disorganized Personality,* McGraw-Hill, New York, 1964, p. 277 f.

7. L. H. Gold, "Psychiatric Profile of the Firesetter," *Journal of Science,* vol. 7, 1962, p. 404.

8. Kisker, *Disorganized Personality,* p. 277 f.

9. M. H. McDowell, Chairman, Dept. of Psychology, Pacific University, Forest Grove, Oregon, in a letter to the author dated Jan. 22, 1970.

10. Cf. chapter 4, where the hero of *Homecoming* also has problems expressed in the freedom-bondage motif.

11. See Alan McGlashan, *The Savage and Beautiful Country,* Chatto & Windus, London, 1966.

12. Harry Levin, *James Joyce: A Critical Introduction,* New Directions, New York, 1958, p. 41.

13. Mishima, *Forbidden Colors,* p. 28.

CHAPTER SIX

1. Yasunari Kawabata, *Japan the Beautiful and Myself,* trans. Edward Seidensticker, Kodansha, Tokyo, 1969, p. 62.

2. Yasunari Kawabata, *House of the Sleeping Beauties and Other Stories,* trans. Edward Seidensticker, Kodansha International, Tokyo, 1969. References are included in the text by page number.

3. Widely quoted. See, for example, *Time,* October 25, 1968, p. 45.

4. George Saito, "Japanese Literature in Western Clothes," *The Oriental Economist,* October 1962, p. 596.

5. Address to the Foreign Teachers of English in Japan, April 20, 1969.

6. My own sampling of university students is inconclusive. Kawabata is read, though not widely. Rarely is he a student's favorite author.

7. Yasunari Kawabata, *Snow Country,* trans. Edward Seidensticker, Knopf, New York, 1956. "One Arm" is a short story included in *House of the Sleeping Beauties and Other Stories.*

8. Edward Seidensticker, introduction to *Snow Country,* p. vii.

9. George Saito, introductory remarks to "The Moon on the Water," *Modern Japanese Stories: An Anthology,* ed. Ivan Morris, Tuttle, Tokyo, 1962, p. 246.

10. Junichiro Tanizaki, *Diary of a Mad Old Man,* trans. Howard Hibbett, Knopf, New York, 1965.

11. Introduction to *House of the Sleeping Beauties and Other Stories,* pp. 7–8.

12. Munesuke Mita, "Patterns of Alienation in Contemporary Japan," *Journal of Social and Political Ideas in Japan* (renamed *The Japan Interpreter*), vol. 5, nos. 2–3, December 1967, p. 149.

13. Ibid., p. 150.

14. Desiderius Erasmus, *The Praise of Folly,* trans. Hoyt Hopewell Hudson, Princeton U. Pr., 1941, pp. 51–52. Cited

in William Willeford's *The Fool and His Scepter,* Northwestern U. Pr., 1969, p. 24.

CHAPTER SEVEN

1. Honor Matthews, *The Hard Journey: The Myth of Man's Rebirth,* Chatto & Windus, London, 1968.

2. Kobo Abe, *The Woman in the Dunes,* trans. E. Dale Saunders, Knopf, New York, 1964. References are included in the text by page number. A film based on the novel was a commercial success and was shown at the International Film Festival in Cannes.

3. Comment on the jacket of the above edition.

4. Donald Keene, "The Artistry of Dazai Osamu," *East-West Review,* vol. 1, 1964–65, pp. 233–53.

5. See Edward Seidensticker, "The Japanese Novel and Disengagement," *Literature and Politics in the Twentieth Century,* ed. G. Mosse and W. Laqueur, Harper & Row, New York, 1967, p. 173.

6. Kobo Abe, *The Face of Another,* trans. E. Dale Saunders, Knopf, New York, 1966; idem, *The Ruined Map,* trans. E. Dale Saunders, Knopf, New York, 1969.

7. See chapter 1, note 27.

8. Comment on the jacket.

9. Charles Baudelaire, *The Room and Other Poems,* trans. C. Day Lewis, Jonathan Cape Ltd., London, 1965. Cited in Matthews's *Hard Journey,* p. 73.

10. Albert Camus's *The Myth of Sisyphus* and, accordingly, *The Stranger* come to mind.

11. Maud Bodkin, *Archetypal Patterns in Poetry,* Knopf, New York, 1958, chap. 4.

12. *The Scarlet Letter.*

CHAPTER EIGHT

1. Kenzaburo Oe, *A Personal Matter,* trans. John Nathan,

Grove Press, New York, 1968. References are included in the text by page number.

2. See, for example, Tadayoshi Sakurai, *Nikudan,* Daitoa Shuppan Kabushiki Kaisha, Tokyo, n.d. This once-popular short book tells "a soldier's story of Port Arthur."

3. As of this writing, Japan is proving a threat to the American textile industry.

4. Abe uses the "map" metaphor in both novels. "His military map, on which enemy and friendly forces were supposed to be clearly defined, was blurred with unknowns" (*The Woman in the Dunes,* p. 224).

5. See Inazo Nitobe, *Bushido: The Soul of Japan,* 1905; Tuttle, Tokyo, 1969.

6. See also pp. 46, 72, 89, 94, 107.

7. Edward Seidensticker, "The Japanese Novel and Disengagement," *Literature and Politics in the Twentieth Century,* ed. G. Mosse and W. Laqueur, Harper and Row, New York, 1967, pp. 177, 183.

8. See also Donald Richie's review of the novel in *The Japan Times,* Wednesday, May 15, 1968.

SYLLABUS
A Suggested Reading Course

The following is a suggested reading guide for students and others who wish either to get acquainted with or improve their knowledge of the postwar Japanese novel, and a course-outline for teachers who wish to introduce Japanese literature to their students. It is based on materials currently available in English, and, needless to say, much that is fine in contemporary Japanese fiction is missing because it has not yet been translated. The user can supplement his reading or teaching as translations become available.

The syllabus is designed for a hypothetical twelve-week "course" in the postwar novel and contains "assigned readings," "collateral readings," and "suggestions for further study." Suggestions are meant to be only that—suggestions—and one could easily adapt the material offered here to suit individual requirements. For example, if used at school, the twelve-week selections could easily be expanded to fit a sixteen-week semester, or otherwise be changed as needs dictated.

Materials chosen are readily available, and the reader who wants to dig deeper will find critical articles and translations scattered throughout various periodicals and other sources, some of which are listed in the Selected Bibliography.

First Week

SUBJECT

Introduction: discussion of the purpose and nature of the course, material to be covered, and some of the features of Japanese literature.

ASSIGNED READINGS

Keene, Donald: *Japanese Literature: An Introduction for Western Readers,* Grove Press, New York, 1955; *Tuttle, Tokyo, 1956.

Yamagiwa, Joseph K.: "Literature and Japanese Culture," *Twelve Doors to Japan,* ed. John W. Hall and Richard K. Beardsley, McGraw-Hill, New York, 1965, chap. 5.

Crisis in Identity, "Crisis in Identity," chap. 1.

COLLATERAL READINGS

Eto, Jun: "An Undercurrent in Modern Japanese Literature," *Journal of Asian Studies,* vol. 23, no. 3, May 1964, pp. 433–45.

Fairbank, John K.; Reischauer, Edwin O.; and Craig, Albert M.: *East Asia: The Modern Transformation,* Houghton Mifflin, "East Asia in the New International World," Boston, 1965, chap. 10; *Tuttle, Tokyo, 1965.

* Asterisks throughout the syllabus indicate editions that are sold only in the Far East.

Ito, Sei: "Modes of Thought in Contemporary Japan," *Japan Quarterly,* vol. 12, 1965, pp. 501–14.

Keene, Donald, ed.: *Anthology of Japanese Literature: Earliest Era to the Mid-Nineteenth Century,* Grove Press, New York, 1955; *Tuttle, Tokyo, 1956.

Reischauer, Edwin: *Japan: The Story of a Nation,* Knopf, New York, 1970; *Tuttle, Tokyo, 1971.

Saito, George: "Japanese Literature in Western Clothes," *The Oriental Economist,* October 1962, pp. 596–97.

Seidensticker, Edward: "Recent and Contemporary Japanese Literature," *The Oriental Economist,* January 1959, pp. 34–35.

Yamagiwa, Joseph K.: "Fiction in Post-War Japan," *Far Eastern Quarterly,* vol. 13, no. 1, November 1953, pp. 3–22.

SUGGESTIONS FOR FURTHER STUDY

1. Speakers: a geographer, for example, could provide an informative and stimulating introduction to Japan's lands and people. Consulates, if nearby, will supply materials and/or guest speakers.

2. *The Tale of Genji* could be divided into sections for reports, with discussion of its features as a novel.

3. Discussion of Japan and analysis of presuppositions or stereotypical attitudes.

4. Correspondence with individuals or a "class secretary" of a Japanese university literature class for future exchange of essays and ideas about particular Japanese novels.

Second Week

SUBJECT

The war in the Pacific: an examination of Japan's literary reaction to involvement and defeat in World War II.

ASSIGNED READINGS

Ooka, Shohei: *Fires on the Plain,* Knopf, New York, 1967; *Tuttle, Tokyo, 1967.

Crisis in Identity, "The War and the Cannibals," chap. 2.

COLLATERAL READINGS

Fairbank, John K.; Reischauer, Edwin O.; and Craig, Albert M.: *East Asia: The Modern Transformation,* "Imperial Japan: from Triumph to Tragedy," Houghton Mifflin, Boston, 1965, chap. 7; *Tuttle, Tokyo, 1965.

Hino, Ashihei: *Barley and Soldiers,* trans. K. and L. W. Bush, Kenkyusha, Tokyo, 1939.

Keene, Donald: "Japanese Writers and the Greater East Asia War," *Journal of Asian Studies,* vol. 23, February 1964, pp. 209–25.

Moriya, Tadashi: *No Requiem,* trans. Geoffrey S. Kishimoto, Hokuseido, Tokyo, 1968.

Oe, Kenzaburo: "The Catch," trans. John Bester, *The Shadow of Sunrise: Selected Stories of Japan and the War,* comp. Shoichi Saeki, Kodansha International, Tokyo, 1966, pp. 15–61.

Takeda, Taijun: *Luminous Moss* in *This Outcast Generation and Luminous Moss,* trans. Yusaburo Shibuya and Sanford Goldstein, Tuttle, Tokyo, 1967.

SUGGESTIONS FOR FURTHER STUDY

1. Reports on anthropological studies of ritual cannibalism will provide ironic background for the literary use of this subject.

2. Montaigne's essay "On the Cannibals" can be read and discussed.

3. A report, or longer study-project, could compare Ooka's novel with Joseph Heller's *Catch-22* in regard to the "madness of war."

4. Comparative studies offer many other possibilities. One might compare *Fires on the Plain* with Hino's *Barley and Soldiers,* written during a time of conquest and victory. Or comparison of American or European war novels and diaries with Japanese accounts would prove stimulating. Norman Mailer's *The Naked and the Dead* would be a natural choice.

5. Journal articles dealing with rationales for and assessments of war could be gathered, discussed, and evaluated. Discussion could include the viability of war as a means of problem-solving in the twentieth century. This would place the week's reading in a broad, philosophical context.

Third Week

SUBJECT

Hiroshima: a consideration of the atomic explosion of 1945 and its literary embodiment.

ASSIGNED READINGS

Ibuse, Masuji: *Black Rain,* trans. John Bester, Kodansha International, Tokyo, 1969.

Crisis in Identity, "After the Bomb," chap. 3.

COLLATERAL READINGS

Agawa, Hiroyuki: *Devil's Heritage,* trans. M. Maki, Hokuseido, Tokyo, 1957.

Fairbank, John K.; Reischauer, Edwin O.; and Craig, Albert M.: *East Asia: The Modern Transformation,* "East Asia in the New International World," Houghton Mifflin, Boston, 1965, chap. 10; *Tuttle, Tokyo, 1965.

Hara, Tamiki: "Summer Flower," trans. George Saito, *The Shadow of Sunrise: Selected Stories of Japan and the War,* comp. Shoichi Saeki, Kodansha International, Tokyo, 1966, pp. 119–31.

Hersey, John: *Hiroshima,* Knopf, New York, 1946.

Jungk, Robert: *Children of the Ashes: The Story of a Rebirth,* trans. Constantine Fitzgibbon, Harcourt, Brace and World, New York, 1961.

Lifton, Robert: *Death in Life: Survivors of Hiroshima,* Random House, New York, 1968.

Pacific War Research Society, comp.: *Japan's Longest Day,* Kodansha International, Tokyo, 1968.

SUGGESTIONS FOR FURTHER STUDY

1. Brief study of map of Hiroshima and the surrounding area, with special reference to places mentioned in *Black Rain.*

2. A factual report of the dropping of the bomb, including statistics of its effects, could accompany a slide presentation and/or pictures of the devastation.

3. Book review of Agawa's *Devil's Heritage*.
4. A report with discussion on Japan's "peace constitution" and the Japan–United States security treaty will point up the impact of the war.
5. Oral report on Yoko Oota's *The City of Corpses* (Kawade Shobo, Tokyo, 1955) and other works dealing with the atomic bombing. See *Synopses of Contemporary Japanese Literature (1936–1955)*, Kokusai Bunka Shinkokai, Tokyo, 1970, pp. 180–82.
6. A wealth of other material is available, for example in *Japan's Longest Day* (see above), which would stimulate many discussions and furnish numerous projects. Topics could range from the negative to the positive, from the effects of radiation burns to the peaceful uses of atomic power.

Fourth Week

Subject

The return: a study of what it means to rediscover one's land and one's self after a period of war or exile.

Assigned Readings

Osaragi, Jiro: *Homecoming,* trans. Brewster Horwitz, Knopf, New York, 1954; *Tuttle, Tokyo, 1955.
Crisis in Identity, "Identity Lost," chap. 4.

Collateral Readings

Ibuse, Masuji: "The Far-Worshipping Commander," trans. Glenn Shaw, *The Shadow of Sunrise: Selected Stories of Japan and the War,* comp. Shoichi Saeki, Kodansha International, 1966, pp. 157–87.

Kawai, Kazuo: *Japan's American Interlude,* University of Chicago Press, Chicago, 1960.

Osaragi, Jiro: *The Journey,* trans. Ivan Morris, Knopf, New York, 1960; *Tuttle, Tokyo, 1960.

"Postwar Social Change" issue of *Journal of Social and Political Ideas in Japan* (renamed *The Japan Interpreter*), vol. 3, no. 3, December 1965.

SUGGESTIONS FOR FURTHER STUDY

1. Oral report or paper giving a brief survey of the history of emperor worship in Japan and suggesting the significance of the emperor's renunciation of his divinity for Japanese cultural life.

2. Discussion of other national cultural symbols such as flag, nation, anthems, famous leaders, and culture heroes. Make lists of American and Japanese (or other national) symbols for comparison. In *Homecoming,* what is Moriya's reaction to the shrines, temples, and cherry blossoms?

3. Report on Tsuneari Fukuda's *The Typhoon Kitty* and Bunroku Shishi's *School of Freedom.* See *Synopses of Contemporary Japanese Literature (1936–1955),* vol. 2, Kokusai Bunka Shinkokai, Tokyo, 1970, pp. 167–70, 176–79.

4. Contrast of prewar and postwar values in reports or discussion of articles in "Postwar Social Change" (see above).

5. Discussion of the "expatriate." America's literary experience following World War I suggests interesting comparisons and contrasts. See for example Frederick J. Hoffman's *The 20's,* especially chapter 2, "The War and the Postwar Temper." See also Malcolm Cowley's *Exiles Return.*

Fifth Week

SUBJECT

Despair: for many, the immediate postwar years were desperate times. A study of the reaction of gloom during the wasteland era.

ASSIGNED READING

Dazai, Osamu: *The Setting Sun,* trans. Donald Keene, New Directions, New York, 1956.

COLLATERAL READINGS

Dazai, Osamu: "The Courtesy Call," trans. Ivan Morris, *Modern Japanese Stories: An Anthology,* ed. Ivan Morris, Tuttle, Tokyo, 1962, pp. 464–80.

———: *No Longer Human,* trans. Donald Keene, New Directions, New York, 1958.

———: "Villon's Wife," trans. Donald Keene, *Modern Japanese Literature: An Anthology,* ed. Donald Keene, Grove Press, New York, 1956, pp. 398–414; *Tuttle, Tokyo, 1957.

Hayashi, Fumiko: "Bones," trans. Ted Takaya, *The Shadow of Sunrise: Selected Stories of Japan and the War,* comp. Shoichi Saeki, Kodansha International, Tokyo, 1966, pp. 133–55.

Keene, Donald: "The Artistry of Dazai Osamu," *East-West Review,* vol. 1, 1964–65, pp. 233–53.

Sakaguchi, Ango: "The Idiot," trans. George Saito, *Modern Japanese Stories,* ed. Morris, pp. 383–415.

Sugiyama, Yoko: "The Waste Land and Contemporary Japanese Poetry," *Comparative Literature,* vol. 13, no. 3, summer 1961, pp. 254–62.

SUGGESTIONS FOR FURTHER STUDY

1. A comparison of *A Streetcar Named Desire* (Tennessee Williams) with *The Setting Sun* to bring out the brittleness and despair of people hungry for love and meaning and who witness and experience their aristocratic tradition disintegrate.

2. A discussion of the concept of identity, including possible definitions and ways in which people define themselves. With regard to *The Setting Sun,* one could discuss the role of tradition in the makeup of one's identity, and what different traditions group members have experienced.

3. As preparation for the above discussion on identity, members could find or compose what they consider to be acceptable definitions of identity.

4. A study of various images of despair and desolation in literature, drawing on members' reading experience. One could start with the "wasteland" image, referring to T. S. Eliot's famous poem.

Sixth Week

SUBJECT

The violent reaction: the postwar period of confusion, emptiness, and crumbling of old value structures produces frustration and dismay. For some of the young it becomes a season of violence.

ASSIGNED READINGS

Ishihara, Shintaro: *Season of Violence and Other Stories,* trans. John G. Mills, Toshie Takahama, and Ken Tremayne, Tuttle, Tokyo, 1966.

COLLATERAL READINGS

Jones, James: *Go to the Widow-Maker,* Delacorte, New York, 1967.

Nozaka, Akiyuki: *The Pornographers,* trans. Michael Gallagher, Secker and Warburg, London, 1969; *Tuttle, Tokyo, 1970.

SUGGESTIONS FOR FURTHER STUDY

1. To the young and dispossessed who wanted to feel "liberated," Ishihara's somewhat sensational works became a kind of inspirational blueprint. One result was the free-wheeling activities of youths referred to as the Sun Tribe. Someone could report on this Japanese phenomenon.

2. An interesting discussion could center on a comparison of the Sun Tribe with America's Hell's Angels.

3. A comparison of James Jones's *Go to the Widow-Maker* with Ishihara's stories in terms of the athletic, sensual approach to life.

4. Reading and discussion of Thom Gunn's poem "On the Move."

5. Analysis of the use of sex and violence in terms of their function in literature; psychological analysis of the same in terms of their being manifestations of protest as well as expressions of need for affirmation. For a recent satiric portrait of the current preoccupation with sex, see Nozaka's *The Pornographers* (see above.)

6. The violence and unrest on campuses in Japan and America in the late 1960s and the beginning of the 1970s suggests numerous possibilities for discussion of the causes, means, and goals of protest.

7. Comparison with works of Nelson Algren.

Seventh Week

SUBJECT

The troubled self: Mishima frequently probes the lives of psychologically disturbed or maladjusted persons trying to understand themselves and their world.

ASSIGNED READINGS

Mishima, Yukio: *The Temple of the Golden Pavilion,* trans. Ivan Morris, Knopf, New York, 1959; *Tuttle, Tokyo, 1959.

Crisis in Identity, "The Creative Quest," chap. 5.

COLLATERAL READINGS

Mishima, Yukio: *After the Banquet,* trans. Donald Keene, Knopf, New York, 1963; *Tuttle, Tokyo, 1963.

————: *Confessions of a Mask,* trans. Meredith Weatherby, New Directions, New York, 1958; *Tuttle, Tokyo, 1970.

————: *Death in Midsummer and Other Stories,* New Directions, New York, 1966.

————: *Five Modern No Plays,* trans. Donald Keene, Knopf, New York, 1957; *Tuttle, Tokyo, 1957.

————: *The Sailor Who Fell from Grace with the Sea,* trans. John Nathan, Knopf, New York, 1965; *Tuttle, Tokyo, 1965.

————: *Thirst for Love,* trans. Alfred H. Marks, Knopf, New York, 1960; *Tuttle, Tokyo, 1970.

————: *Forbidden Colors,* trans. Alfred H. Marks, Knopf, New York, 1968, *Tuttle, Tokyo, 1969.

SUGGESTIONS FOR FURTHER STUDY

1. The availability of Mishima's works in English suggests that a number of comparative studies or reports on individual works would be profitable.
2. Edward Albee's *Who's Afraid of Virginia Woolf* and *The Zoo Story* would make interesting comparative studies (with Mishima) of the schizophrenic modern spirit. *The Zoo Story* could be read aloud in the group and later discussed in comparison with *The Temple of the Golden Pavilion.*
3. A discussion and analysis of Theodore Roethke's poem "In a Dark Time."
4. Guest lecture on schizophrenia by a psychologist.
5. Discussion of the role of the artist in fiction, the "artist-novel" (*Künstlerroman*), and autobiographical fiction in general, especially in relation to the Japanese "I-novel" tradition.

Eighth Week

SUBJECT

Crisis of faith: the disaffection with traditional religious frames of reference and the search for new affirmations.

ASSIGNED READING

Endo, Shusaku: *Silence,* trans. William Johnston, Tuttle, Tokyo, 1969.

COLLATERAL READINGS

Bunce, William K., ed.: *Religions in Japan,* Tuttle, Tokyo, 1955.

Endo, Shusaku: "Fuda no Tsuji," trans. Frank Hoff and James Kirkup, *Japan P.E.N. News,* no. 14, January 1965, pp. 1–9.

Gallagher, Michael: "A Japanese-Catholic Novel," *Commonweal,* vol. 85, pp. 136–38.

Mathy, Francis: "Shusaku Endo: Japanese Catholic Novelist," *Thought,* vol. 47, 1967, pp. 585–614.

Niwa, Fumio: *The Buddha Tree,* trans. Kenneth Strong, Owen, London, 1966; *Tuttle, Tokyo, 1966.

Shiina, Rinzo: "Midnight Banquet," trans. Noah Brannen, *Trans Pacific,* no. 3, 1970, pp. 33–45.

Thomsen, Harry: *The New Religions of Japan,* Tuttle, Tokyo, 1963.

SUGGESTIONS FOR FURTHER STUDY

1. A comparison of Arthur Miller's *The Crucible* with Endo's *Silence* might stimulate discussion concerning various features of faith under duress.

2. Many books and other materials are available (see above) concerning Japan's intriguing "new religions." Reports could be made on two of the largest, Soka Gakkai and Rissho Koseikai.

3. Philip Larkin's poem "Church Going" in *The Less Deceived* could provide a basis for discussion concerning the adequacy of traditional symbols.

4. A wide range of reports, projects, or discussions could probe the contemporary "death of God" theology and provide points of contact with *Silence.* Books like Harvey Cox's *The Secular City* and works by Hamilton and other "death of God" theologians should prove useful.

5. A guest expert on Japanese religions could provide some useful background on the influence of Buddhism and other religions on Japanese culture.

Ninth Week

SUBJECT

Metaphysical dilemma: contemporary man frequently feels trapped, isolated, and burdened with anxiety. His quest for meaning often takes him on a journey through labyrinths of doubt.

ASSIGNED READINGS

Abe, Kobo: *The Woman in the Dunes,* trans. E. Dale Saunders, Knopf, New York, 1964; *Tuttle, Tokyo, 1964.

Crisis in Identity, "Identity Found," chap. 7.

COLLATERAL READINGS

Abe, Kobo: *The Face of Another,* trans. E. Dale Saunders, Knopf, New York, 1966; *Tuttle, Tokyo, 1966.

———: "Red Cocoon," trans. John Nathan, *Japan Quarterly,* vol. 13, April/June, 1966, pp. 217–19.

———: *The Ruined Map,* trans. E. Dale Saunders, Knopf, New York, 1969; *Tuttle, Tokyo, 1970.

———: "Stick," trans. John Nathan, *Japan Quarterly,* vol. 13, April/June 1966, pp. 214–17.

Korges, James: "Abe and Ooka: Identity and Mind–Body," *Critique,* vol. 10, no. 2, pp. 130–48.

Matthews, Honor: *The Hard Journey: The Myth of Man's Rebirth,* Chatto and Windus, London, 1968.

Schultz, Beth: Book review of *The Woman in the Dunes*, *The East-West Review*, vol. 2, no. 1, spring/summer 1965, pp. 77–82.

SUGGESTIONS FOR FURTHER STUDY

1. Members could gather definitions of "existentialism," compare various features, and prepare a satisfactory working definition as a basis for discussing novels. Is Abe's novel "existentialist"?

2. Numerous works deal with contemporary man's frustrations when confronted with meaninglessness and absurdity. Comparisons might be made between Abe and others like Kafka, Camus, Sartre, Beckett, and Brecht.

3. A discussion of "trappedness" as a phenomenon of contemporary literature. What images of "trappedness" appear? One of the most common is the prison. Cf. works of Kafka, Camus, and Sartre, for example. What features of society produce the protagonists' feelings of despair or frustration?

4. A group reading of a portion of Chagall's play *The Typists* or of Sartre's *No Exit*.

Tenth Week

SUBJECT

Reclaiming the past: a consideration of the significance and continuity of tradition and its conflict with the present.

ASSIGNED READING

Tanizaki, Junichiro: *The Makioka Sisters*, trans. Edward Seidensticker, Knopf, New York, 1957; *Tuttle, Tokyo, 1958.

COLLATERAL READINGS

Keene, Donald: *Modern Japanese Novels and the West,* U. of Virginia Pr., Charlottesville, 1961.

———, ed. and trans.: *The Old Woman, the Wife, and the Archer,* Viking, New York, 1961.

Hibbett, Howard, S.: "Tradition and Trauma in the Contemporary Japanese Novel," *Daedalus,* vol. 95, pp. 925–40.

Mishima, Yukio: *The Sound of Waves,* trans. Meredith Weatherby, Knopf, New York, 1956; *Tuttle, Tokyo, 1956.

Nagai, Kafu: *Geisha in Rivalry,* trans. Kurt Meissner and Ralph Friedrich, Tuttle, Tokyo, 1963.

Tanizaki, Junichiro: *The Key,* trans. Howard Hibbett, Knopf, New York, 1961; *Tuttle, Tokyo, 1971.

———: *Seven Japanese Tales,* trans. Howard Hibbett, Knopf, New York, 1963; *Tuttle, Tokyo, 1963.

SUGGESTIONS FOR FURTHER STUDY

1. The role of the past: a comparison (either in papers or discussion) of attitudes toward the past. Americans can look back only to the colonial era, unless they take the English tradition into account. Japanese can look to the fifth or sixth century. What features of the past remain significant? How do Japan and the United States differ in this respect?

2. Conflict of past and present. The "generation gap" is currently a popular expression. In what ways does Tanizaki's novel reflect different attitudes toward the traditional and the modern?

3. Report on *miai,* the role of the go-between, and an ex-

amination of different cultural traditions regarding marriage.

4. The famous geisha tradition has undergone significant change. A report on this tradition, especially in connection with Nagai's novel, would prove interesting.

5. A film or, better, a performance of Bunraku, Kyogen, Noh, or Kabuki drama would be fascinating as a sampling of Japan's traditional dramatic forms.

Eleventh Week

SUBJECT

Last extremity: old age and approaching death. A pondering of the ways in which men strive to cope with the inevitable.

ASSIGNED READINGS

Kawabata, Yasunari: *House of the Sleeping Beauties and Other Stories,* trans. Edward Seidensticker, Kodansha International, Tokyo, 1969.

Crisis in Identity, "The Last Extremity," chap. 6.

COLLATERAL READINGS

Kawabata, Yasunari: *Japan the Beautiful and Myself,* trans. Edward Seidensticker, Kodansha International, Tokyo, 1969.

———: "The Moon on the Water," trans. George Saito, *Modern Japanese Stories: An Anthology,* ed. Ivan Morris, Tuttle, Tokyo, 1962, pp. 245–57.

———: *Snow Country,* trans. Edward Seidensticker, Knopf, New York, 1955; *Tuttle, Tokyo, 1955.

————: *Thousand Cranes,* trans. Edward Seidensticker, Knopf, New York, 1959; *Tuttle, Tokyo, 1959.

Maeda, Cana: "On Translating the *Haiku* Form," *Harvard Journal of Asiatic Studies,* vol. 29, 1969, pp. 131–68.

Niwa, Fumio: "The Hateful Age," trans. Ivan Morris, *Modern Japanese Stories,* ed. Morris, pp. 320–48.

Tanizaki, Junichiro: *Diary of a Mad Old Man,* trans. Howard Hibbett, Knopf, New York, 1965; *Tuttle, Tokyo, 1965.

Yasuda, Ken: *The Japanese Haiku: Its Essential Nature, History, and Possibilities in English with Selected Examples,* Tuttle, Tokyo, 1957.

SUGGESTIONS FOR FURTHER STUDY

1. Reading and discussion of Kawabata's Nobel prize acceptance speech.
2. Study of the *haiku* tradition in Japanese literature, with reference to its influence on Kawabata's work.
3. Writing of *haiku* in English.
4. Report on Niwa's "The Hateful Age" and discussion of the problems of old age. A sociologist could provide a stimulating analysis.
5. Hemingway's *The Old Man and the Sea* would make an interesting comparison with *House of the Sleeping Beauties* and *Diary of a Mad Old Man.*

Twelfth Week

SUBJECT

The contemporary hero: a look at the modern concepts of hero and antihero and a comparison with the past.

Syllabus: Reading Course

ASSIGNED READINGS

Oe, Kenzaburo: *A Personal Matter,* trans. John Nathan, Grove Press, New York, 1968; *Tuttle, Tokyo, 1969. *Crisis in Identity,* "A New Hero," chap. 8.

COLLATERAL READINGS

Hayashi, Fumiko: "Downtown,," trans. Ivan Morris, *Modern Japanese Stories: An Anthology,* ed. Ivan Morris, Tuttle, Tokyo, 1962, pp. 349–64.

Nitobe, Inazo: *Bushido: The Soul of Japan,* 1905; Tuttle, Tokyo, 1969.

Oe, Kenzaburo: "Lavish are the Dead," trans. John Nathan, *Japan Quarterly,* vol. 12, April/June 1965, pp. 193–211.

Seidensticker, Edward: "The Japanese Novel and Disengagement," *Literature and Politics in the Twentieth Century,* ed. G. Mosse and W. Lacqueur, Harper and Row, New York, 1967, pp. 169–86.

SUGGESTIONS FOR FURTHER STUDY

1. A useful review of the course might be undertaken by a comparison of the various kinds of heroes presented. What qualities do they display? Does any clear picture of modern "heroic" qualities emerge?

2. A report on Japan's famous tale of the forty-seven *ronin* and discussion of the concept of loyalty as presented there in contrast with contemporary novels.

3. Oe's *A Personal Matter* invites comparison with some contemporary American works, such as those of Updlike, Bellow, and Salinger. In what ways is Oe's hero similar to and different from Updike's protagonist in *Rabbit Run?*

4. A discussion of the concept of the antihero. What are his qualities? Cf. Willie Loman in Arthur Miller's *Death of a Salesman*.

5. A paper comparing several of the novels in the syllabus in terms of some common theme, such as love, death, or isolation.

SELECTED BIBLIOGRAPHY

The student, teacher, or general reader who wishes to read more extensively will find the following basic sources helpful.

BIBLIOGRAPHIES

Japan P.E.N. Club: *Japanese Literature in European Languages: A Bibliography,* Japan P.E.N. Club, Tokyo, 1961. Supplement, 1964. Essential. Has the advantage of periodical supplements which appear in *The Japan P.E.N. News.*

Journal of Asian Studies: Annual bibliography of Asian Studies.

Nunn, G. Raymond: *East Asia: A Bibliography of Bibliographies,* East-West Center, University of Hawaii, Honolulu, 1967. Occasional Paper no. 7. Includes Japanese and Western language sources under a wide range of topics.

Publication of the Modern Language Association (PMLA): Annual bibliography of Asian Studies.

Silberman, Bernard S: *Japan and Korea: A Critical Bibliography,* University of Arizona Press, Tucson, 1962. A basic and fairly complete listing for the period covered.

SELECTED FICTION

Japan P.E.N. Club News: Japan P.E.N. Club, Room 265, Shuwa Residential Hotel, 1–7, Akasaka 9–chome, Minato-ku, Tokyo. Issues contain translations of short stories and poems, as well as synopses.

Japan Quarterly: Japan Publications Trading Co., P. O. Box 5030, Tokyo International, Tokyo. Translations, book reviews, and critical essays.

Modern Japanese Literature: From 1868 to the Present Day, compiled and edited by Donald Keene, Grove Press, New York, 1956; in the Far East, Charles E. Tuttle, Tokyo, 1957. Included in the Syllabus as a supplementary text.

Modern Japanese Stories: An Anthology, edited by Ivan Morris, Charles E. Tuttle, Rutland, Vermont, and Tokyo, Japan, 1962. The best single collection of short stories.

The Shadow of Sunrise: Selected Stories of Japan and the War, selected by Shoichi Saeki, Kodansha International, Tokyo, 1966. Five stories. A fine collection.